Scribe Publications
NEO POWER

The authors are joint directors of the privately funded consumer think-tank, the Centre for Customer Strategy.

Consumer behaviourist Ross Honeywill became an internationally recognised authority on the impact on Australia of a rapidly changing social fabric through his leadership role at KPMG (Asia Pacific) between 1997 and 2001. As a business strategist, he has played a central role in large-scale transformation projects for global brands. Prior to working at KPMG, Ross was a senior executive for national retail brands. He has won business and marketing awards in the tourism, property development, telecommunications, and retail sectors.

A respected social scientist, Verity Byth led the research and consumer analysis that underpins the NEO typology. Her professional experience ranges across industries from airlines and banking to tourism and retailing. Consumer insights director of the privately funded consumer think-tank the Centre for Customer Strategy, Ms Byth designs and leads all its research projects, including market-testing and development of brand strategies, marketing, and creative executions, and NEO consumer insights.

www.neogroup.net <http://www.neogroup.net>

neo
power

how the new economic order is
changing the way we live, work, and play

Ross Honeywill & Verity Byth

SCRIBE
Melbourne

Scribe Publications Pty Ltd
PO Box 523
Carlton North, Victoria, Australia 3054
Email: info@scribepub.com.au

First published by Scribe 2006

Typeset in 11.5/16 pt Baskerville
Cover design by Peter Long
Printed and bound in Australia by Griffin Press

National Library of Australia
Cataloguing-in-Publication data

Honeywill, Ross.
NEO power : how the new economic order is changing the way we live,
work, and play.

ISBN 1 921215 02 X.
1. Generation Y - Australia. 2. Intergenerational relations - Australia.
3. Australia - Social conditions - 2001- . I. Byth, Verity. II. Title.

305.20994

www.scribepub.com.au

Contents

Preface

The New Social Compass

'It is better to light a candle than to rage against the darkness.'
Chinese Proverb

Australians used to understand what was going on, but somehow it got away from them in the nineties as the Information Age turned the tried-and-true on its head. They found themselves buried under a landslide of information that was often meaningless. Labels such as generation X, generation Y, baby boomer, and ABs are, for example, useless in describing our desires, or in explaining how and why we behave as complex human beings.

To find an answer, the authors spent five years surveying 500,000 respondents, and discovered that a revolutionary breed is charting a new course and changing the world.

This landmark analysis reveals startling new evidence that four million Australians are transforming their social and political landscape by redefining the economic fabric of the nation. Change is occurring in the corridors of power and on local street corners alike as traditional ways are abandoned by personally powerful individuals who inhabit the world of new information technology.

This influential band, known as the new economic order, or NEO, provides us with a new social compass that makes immediate sense of a confused world.

However, first things first. In the late 1990s, we identified a significant gap in the available measures of customer value. Typically, customer-value measurements or metrics include individual wealth, socio-economic profiling (income, occupation, and education), and enterprise-based transaction records. You will get no argument from us that income is important—a consumer must have money to be able to spend it—but the surprising news is that those with money don't automatically have any desire to part with it.

Two problems exist, therefore, with net worth and socio-economics as effective measures of value. The first is that they rely on savings or income rather than spending; the second is that they offer nothing on the personality or psychology of the consumer. For example, why do people spend money? What will motivate them to spend? Do they even want to spend?

There are also two problems with transactional or spending data within a specific enterprise or corporation. The first is that the data only relates to that enterprise and provides no insight into what a customer is doing elsewhere—particularly with competitors. The second problem, once again, is that it offers nothing on the personality or psychology of the consumer.

Qualitative metrics, on the other hand, provide much more information about the attitudes and values of consumers, but provide no quantified data on spending—either spending behaviour or spending capacity.

It is worth mentioning here that spending models do exist. And it is widely recognised that high-spenders behave differently from low-spenders. What form that behavioural difference takes and what motivates different consumption behaviours has, until now, remained a mystery.

Having identified and defined the parameters of the knowledge gap, we set about creating and testing a solution. In closing the gap, we used four data sources and four modelling methodologies over a period of seven years.

In 2001, we formed an alliance with Roy Morgan Research internationally in order to have access to a stable database with global reach. In doing so, we streamlined the development process and took advantage of the 2,000-plus variables in the Roy Morgan Single Source environment. We applied our NEO algorithms to Roy Morgan's Single Source data to provide a robust view of the economy's most valuable consumers.

Two final challenges remained. The first was to create a typology that not only had rich attitudinal data (the NEO typology has 84 attitudinal factors) necessary for practical marketing activities. The second was to ensure that the typology had the rich behavioural data (the NEO typology has 100 behavioural factors) essential for attributing or identifying the most valuable consumers on a customer database or existing customer segments.

The result is a unique measure of high-yield consumption drawn from 120,000 respondents each year across four continents. The specific output from this process is a new measure of psychological characteristics and spending propensity, produced in line with Roy Morgan International's global quality and production protocols. We have applied the new customer metric to data in the USA, Australia, New Zealand, the UK, and Indonesia. Soon, we will be applying it to China and India as well.

In a transforming society, power comes to those who successfully recognise who is charting the new path. This book provides the lens necessary to identify and track the cross-generational band of Australians mapping that path. It has been written utilising a bedrock of vast consumer research to identify the fascinating and revolutionary changes in society that will make a difference to every reader. It provides a fresh framework for fathoming the future.

This book demonstrates that new rules apply in understanding how consumption arousal is changing society. So let's begin the journey by setting the new compass. Along the way, we'll explore how Australia is being shaped by NEOs and how a social evolution is establishing, under our noses, a transformed society.

Let the journey begin.

Introduction

The Path Less Travelled

'Give me the options and I'll always take the path less travelled.'
Bob Geldoff

The workers and consumers who make up the new economic order or NEO are socially progressive, economically conservative, and hungry for rich information and memorable experiences. They defy cultural clichés such as generation X or Y, and every day set about changing their world by expressing their differences.

NEO behaviour is based not on a desire for *things* alone, but on the unique personal meaning of *things* to each individual consumer. Swiss jeweller Otto Kunsli created in 1980 a matt-black rubber bracelet titled *Gold Makes You Blind*. The bracelet has, under its black rubber exterior, a secret cache of pure gold. Only the wearer, and those in the know, are aware there is gold beneath the matt rubber. This is inconspicuous consumption in the extreme. This is tertiary consumption where symbols and *passwords* outrank the mere objectivity of things. This is the NEO world of whispered secrets.

Imagination, creativity, and desire combine at the heart of this social and economic transformation. Tertiary consumption enters the realms of ethics and principles, of a rewarding experience filled with rich information and exciting secrets. NEOs are different in every way to more traditional Australians.

In the NEO, personal productivity has become more relevant than the mass production of goods and the delivery of basic services. In this NEO universe, objects keep their practical utility but also convert into signs or symbols of meaning. Objects are transformed into symbols that convey messages, not just about themselves but also about the people who value them, the people who consume them. They become symbols of desire.

The NEO is the new social and economic vocabulary. This is where basic things carry vastly less value than the symbols that have risen in their place—than experiences and discretionary choices.

The members of this revolutionary band are challenging and abandoning the traditional ways.

They are defined by their progressive social attitudes, tertiary consumption, personal experiences, and evolving relationships.

Conversely, traditional Australians are aroused only by basic needs and the demand for rudimentary satisfaction. Traditional Australia is rooted in social, industrial, and technological conservatism; it is defined by traditional values and by the production and exchange of objects.

With half the Australian population in the traditional or basic-needs group, is it any wonder that discount store brands such as Harvey Norman and Target are thriving? For the eight million Traditionals, consumption arousal is triggered by a deal: just like a politician offering lower taxes in return for a vote, or a retailer offering an unbeatable deal on a familiar brand, with easy payment terms and a sense of urgency. Target and its competitor Harvey Norman understand this deal-mentality and the basic-needs consumption patterns of the market majority.

The traditional mode of behaviour is driven by the interplay between basic needs, consumer demand, and the transactional deal. And this is where most social commentators and marketers start and finish. Conventional approaches to consumer behaviour recognise only those satisfied by this basic response to fundamental needs; assuming that everyone behaves in a more-or-less standard and standardised way.

Similarly, lifestage constructs like generation X or Y and the baby boomer label tell us nothing about how and why people behave. Nor do they foretell the future.

Traditional Australia frequently looks and behaves in one community, one industry sector, or one consumer market pretty much as it does in another. It has its roots in the mass marketing and mass media model that influenced most of the twentieth century. This was the ironically named modernist era of primary (agrarian) and secondary (industrial) mass production, mass media, and mass marketing. And now in the late stages of the homogeneous era, good and evil, right and wrong, left and right have all become indistinguishable as political parties simulate each other and the media simulates reality.

In the twenty-first century, we have a different strand of society, a new powerhouse driver of the economy. Sitting well beyond either primary or secondary levels of demand, the tertiary attitudes and behaviours of this new economic order are driven by deep desire and the search for creative self-recognition and imaginative self-definition.

The new economic order is generating a new self-governing, self-defining NEO-Modernist framework in a world of otherwise random decision-making. NEOs are reinventing their world—at work, home, and play—and they are creating a groundswell that is polarising society, culture, and global business strategy.

Suddenly, we can fashion our own future by making sense of the changing world.

Welcome to the path less travelled.

PART ONE
Planet NEO

True North

A revolutionary change is occurring in Australia. A new economic order is redefining the fabric of our social and economic lives.

Members of this new economic order, or NEO, read more, are better educated than the rest of the population, vote for the coalition but prefer the progressive social policies of the Greens, like football but love the arts, devour the Internet, believe food is a celebration of the day, drink more wine but still love a beer, earn more and spend more than other Australians, and demand more from just about everyone.

If this sounds like you and four million of your closest friends, you are reinventing Australia. And, whereas eight million of your more conservative cousins known as Traditionals allow doctors, bank managers, bureaucrats, power utilities, local governments, and telephone companies to dictate decisions in their best interests, NEOs will decide what is best for them.

When the new economic order emerged as a force in 1991, a new social 'wave' began its ascendancy across the globe. It gathered up in its wake all the values and aspirations of NEOs and began shifting society from a traditional or institutional way of life to a decidedly individual focus.

Traditionals and NEOs aspire to different lives, and this makes for a country split in two.

NEOs seek out the fresh Italian white truffle pasta at Icebergs Dining Room and Bar at Bondi while those all around them are looking for an inexpensive and satisfying bowl of mushroom soup or a ready-to-go sandwich.

While NEOs are in the minority they fight way above their weight in the power they exert on society, outweighing all the numerical muscle of Traditionals. These two fundamentally different types live side by side in a changed world that has fewer rules and more power for each individual willing to embrace the change.

NEOs rule in the post-corporate, post-institutional era in which individual power is replacing institutional power. On any day in the great cities of the world, NEOs are actively rejecting the influence of the traditional gatekeepers of authority such as bureaucrats, bank managers, and doctors. Instead, they are putting authority back in individual hands.

We are all impacted by this seismic social activity. The signs are clear and observable across the globe. In the Philippines, Indonesia, South America, Fiji, and South Korea, governments continuously run the gauntlet of local democracy. Yes, it is disruptive and unpredictable, but that is the nature of individuals forming brief but powerful coalitions or communities of polar interest, and wreaking change on those who have forgotten who put them there in the first place.

It is not only in the world's hot spots that we experience this personal, anti-institutional, anti-equilibrium muscle. In Liverpool, England, home to the Beatles and a site of former industrial might, a Democracy Commission was born out of a formidable coalition of local interests. It set about persuading elected officials to give back some of the rates and taxes sufficient, at least, to fund individual decisions on local improvements in individual wards or precincts. We can see examples of this people power—or the reclaiming of individual authority and influence—around every corner.

In America, areas known as 'business improvement districts' are giving individuals a greater say in their local neighbourhood. For example, in New York City, local residents and small businesses created the Bryant Park Restoration Corporation to rehabilitate a derelict and dangerous public site. Now, on balmy summer nights, they screen open-air movies, with visitors sitting on loose seating that can be moved around to suit the viewer. The individual seat, a small but significant symbol of the devolution of power, has replaced the fixed bench of the urban bureaucrat.

Elsewhere in the US, the Dudley Street neighbourhood, once Boston's most impoverished area, is living proof of how a resident-led initiative can rebuild a community. Peter Medoff and Holly Sklar revealed in their book *Streets of Hope* that the rebirth of this neglected neighbourhood was shaped by the dreams of ordinary people of different races and generations.

We see and hear this influence that occurs on an individual level every day in our own lives—on talkback radio, in the polls that politicians find so seductive, and in the local planning decisions that are beginning to reflect the will of local residents over the corporation looking for a fast profit at the expense of community interests. The signs, the symbols of change, indicate that NEOs are reclaiming the reins; they are not prepared to accept the traditional rules of politics, business, or religion.

Throughout the 1980s and 1990s economists embraced the principles of globalisation and, while riding the crest of the institutional or traditional wave, witnessed the long boom. But they failed to take adequate account of the undercurrent of social and economic change that would render the boom nothing more than unaffordable good fortune. Traditional ways of behaving — *institutional* ways — would not be enough as the new economic order grew in strength. Most missed its emergence, confusing social change with the arrival of new technology, and many continue to fail to grasp its social and economic significance.

Coincidental with the NEO wave of change, the future of an institutionalised or globalised world is now looking less certain than it did at the turn of the millennium. The shift to vast economic unions and the dream of a shared prosperity were deeply wounded when EU members voted against issues that threatened their own sovereignty and when the Soviet Union reorganised into nation states. Individualism became increasingly entrenched across the globe.

The world was experiencing a shift from the blunt instrument of institutionalism and globalism to the sharp determinism of the individual.

Emergence

It was the advent of the Information Age in 1991 that cata-pulted NEOs into their new place in the world — their personal landscape of self-determination and self-realisation, of the handmade, of brand relationships — and their journey of desire, discovery, and reward.

In *Intellectual Capital: the new wealth of organization,* American author Thomas Stewart identifies the beginning of the Information Age as 1991 when US companies spent more on information technology than on production technology: $US112 billion on machines to gather, process, and distribute information, well ahead of the $US107 billion spent on machines to make and move physical objects.

The late Pope John-Paul II also invoked a blessing on this changing world. Australian writer Peter Hartcher observed that in 1991 the Pope declared in his *Centesimus Annus* that, while the decisive factor of production used to be land and capital, it is now knowledge.

This rare convergence of the Pope's blessing and the Information Age signalled that seismic change had begun.

Coincidental with these changes, Australia was staggering out of the depths of one of the worst economic recessions since the Second World War. Overnight, companies folded, and people's dreams and livelihoods evaporated. And when the nightmare ended, we found that, during this wintry darkness, many of us had changed forever. We came out of the recession with a different take on the world. The old and established patterns of behaviour were no longer relevant. Many wanted a new world—and NEOs set about creating it.

International socio-economic studies showed that at the beginning of the 1990s around 30 per cent of women in France and Italy had a post-modern outlook, as did approximately 25 per cent in the Netherlands. This finding corresponds directly with the international population percentages of NEOs—that band of quintessentially NEO-modern individuals.

During the 1990s Paul Ray and Sherry Gardner conducted a US social study and in 2000 published a book identifying a group of 50 million Americans whom the authors called *Cultural Creatives*. The social and psychological characteristics of *Cultural Creatives* are remarkably similar to those of the NEO. In the US there are 59 million NEOs.

The weight of international evidence is compelling. Society is changing, and the changes are all around us.

Difference

It is, however, at the personal level that the seminal differences appear so stark.

NEOs are as different from Traditional Australians as diamonds and coal, but their differences and individuality do not mean they cannot be recognised and identified. In fact, it is their individuality that helps us to identify and understand them.

NEOs vote with their feet. They will leave a restaurant if it isn't up to scratch. They will dump a telephone company because they receive a 'Dear Sir/Madam' note rather than a personally addressed letter. A NEO will insist that her doctor provide background reading on a diagnosis—and she will then seek a second opinion.

NEOs will move from one employer to another because the first, failing to recognise the difference between leadership and management, simply will not deal with their individuality. And, although they consume more than anyone else, they will only consume when and where they feel they are being treated as individuals. A NEO will pay a premium for special treatment as an individual and for quality, design, and a personalised experience.

NEOs exhibit 194 robust, strongly discriminating attitudinal, behavioural, and spending characteristics. These are the traits that make them individually powerful, complex, and compelling.

A Movado watch and a Rolex, for example, convey very different messages about their wearers. Both are wristwatches, both function perfectly and keep time without error, but their symbolic value bears no relationship to their functional or constructed value as mere objects. The Movado, exhibited in New York's Museum of Modern Art, is an imaginative symbol of a modern design aesthetic; the Rolex, a symbol of traditional wealth and status. The Movado is a symbol of the NEO Australian; the Rolex, of the traditional Australian.

Traditionals feel they can't make much of a difference on

their own. And so, unlike NEOs, they surrender decision-making to others, attracted as they are by the certainty of global brands—those reassuring symbols of the big companies they grew up with and that are reminders of the way things used to be.

Life for Traditionals sees fate playing the hand. But the flipside of this reliance on luck takes Traditionals into the realm of gaming and bargain hunting, where even small windfalls deliver large levels of satisfaction.

We are all familiar with the story of the man who drives all the way across town to save a few cents a litre on a tank of petrol. The conventional wisdom is that it costs him more to cover all that distance than he saves buying the cheaper petrol. It is told to illustrate how illogically he is behaving. But what the anecdote doesn't capture is that it's not important that the driver didn't make a saving. What matters most to him is that he got the best price. Life for a Traditional is not driven by economics; it's more concerned with achieving small wins against the odds.

Traditional Australians are also very security conscious, and place a high value on certainty; so once they have a job, they stick with it rather than risk a change. And they are unlikely to ask for a raise or a promotion—it's just too risky. Traditionals like to be employed and to stay employed. A Traditional defines himself by his job—it's not only what he does, it's also who he is.

Traditionals also define themselves by the brands they acquire to give meaning to their lives. For example, when a Traditional buys a BMW, it is for the badge and the status it represents; for the status message it sends to those around him. A Traditional surrounds himself with established brands and then defines himself by the 'brand halo'.

And while they try to keep up with life's rapid changes, all the technological transformations in contemporary life are just another set of unwelcome changes to be endured by Traditional Australians. Banks in the late 1970s introduced automated teller machines (ATMs) to their street frontages and promoted them in an attempt to move Traditionals away from the counters staffed by high-cost tellers. However, the banks had not taken account of their low tolerance to change and their high resistance to new technology. The result? The low-value Traditionals stayed in the expensive banking chamber while the high-value NEOs were quick to accept the changes and new technology, and were delighted that they no longer had to enter a bank to transact their business.

Years later, banks still struggle with the dilemma of low-value customers clogging their costly counters. It even appears that some actively reduce counter staff in peak periods to make queues longer and longer in an attempt to push those pesky Traditionals out into the street where the low-cost ATM awaits them. Most banks now charge fees for counter transactions to dissuade Traditionals from entering the banking chamber at all.

Understanding how NEOs feel about technology is more complex given that, on the one hand, they want Internet and telephone banking that enables them to avoid going into a bank branch at all; on the other hand, they insist on personal engagement with their financial planner. This requires an understanding of the difference between a pure transaction and the technology that enables engagement or invites emotional involvement.

Traditionals are happy with institutions—they love shopping malls and, while the concrete canyons of large cities daunt them, they are comforted by the familiar logos sitting atop the skyscrapers. They relish 'events' and many will go into debt to buy that special gift for the family at Christmas, on Mothers' Day, or Valentines' Day. And they love sale events more than anything else. Forget location, location, location. For a Traditional, the slogan is *price, price, price*. Add a dash of urgency and you have consumption arousal, Traditional style.

Individuals in the new economic order, on the other hand, dislike the sameness of shopping malls, and visit them only when they have to. They prefer the human scale of hip strips and urban villages. In the urban village or NEO neighbour-hood, NEOs will be reading more books, eating out, and drinking more wine than Traditionals.

When NEOs buy a BMW, they communicate clear messages, not to others, but rather to themselves: whispered secrets on desire, beauty, safety, design quality, and a sense of reward for simply making it through another year. This is inconspicuous consumption that speaks, not to the crowd about prestige and status, but to the soul of the individual consumer about himself or herself.

We have now found NEOs, and NEOs have found their true north and are changing the world. We can now choose whether or not we change with them.

NEOs: a snapshot

You may be drawing a mental picture of an upmarket, elite group with more money than practical sense. That is a mistake. Remember, NEOs are far from some small niche in society—they are a quarter of the population, and have powerful social and economic clout. They will buy new technology—all those 3G mobile phones, wireless laptops, wireless Broadband, iPods, digital cameras, and wireless scanners—but they'll also spend their hard-won rewards on home extensions and renovations, travel, eating in and out, drinking, banking, investing, and an entire range of services that make their lives easier, more individual, and more controllable. They'll vote governments in and out, fill our universities, take professional roles and executive positions, and shape society.

But who are the people who populate this new economic order?

To qualify as a NEO, a consumer must have both:

- High levels of spending (past, present, and intended)—they must score in the top 25 per cent of twelve discretionary-spending factors and ...

- High scores (and high discrimination) in both the underlying attitudes that motivate high spending, and the behavioural activities that signpost spending motivation—they must be in the top 40 per cent of the 184 NEO attitudinal and behavioural factors.

Society is split pretty much in two. The Traditional half of the population exhibit conservative social attitudes, low spending, and low-discretionary-choice behaviour.

They are price-sensitive and more interested in a *deal* than in *quality*. As a consequence, they account for only 23 per cent of all discretionary spending.

The other half consists of high-spending, high-discretionary-choice NEOs and another group known as Evolvers, who may score well on NEO characteristics but may not currently spend enough to qualify them as part of the new economic order. If either their spending or behavioural score increases sufficiently, they will be classified as NEOs—hence the name Evolvers. Between them, NEOs and Evolvers account for 77 per cent of discretionary spending.

In addition to the four million NEOs in Australia, there are 750,000 in New Zealand, 12 million in the UK, and 59 million in the USA.

A NEO is born a NEO and, depending on circumstances throughout his or her life, will always be either a NEO or an Evolver. A Traditional is born a Traditional and will die a Traditional. There is no migration between one half of the population and the other.

A word of warning about self-assessment. In determining whether they are NEOs or Traditionals, many people become confused about apparent conflicts or contrasts in their behaviour and attitudes that seem to cross over from one type to the other. We often hear comments such as, 'I think I'm a NEO, but I behave like a Traditional when it comes to getting the best deal from a telephone company or from a bank on a credit card.'

Determining whether you are a NEO or a Traditional requires a detailed assessment, so guessing can be counter-productive. That said, readers will begin to form a generalised view of where their behaviours and attitudes lie. So, as apparent contradictions arise, remember they may well be just that: apparent. To take the example given above, a NEO behaves in exactly the same way as a Traditional when price is the only factor in a brand's value proposition. Most telephone companies and credit-card providers have allowed their products to be viewed simply as commodities offered at a price. And given that, typically, there is no emotion or involvement in a commodity purchase, we all behave in ways that are very similar. It's only when desire or emotion enters the transaction that the differences between NEOs and Traditionals surface.

A good example is the liquor retail brand Dan Murphy's, which operates principally on low prices and high volume. Both Traditionals and NEOs shop at Dan Murphy's because of its low prices. A NEO may therefore confuse this with Traditional behaviour. However, there are fundamental differences in how both types shop. The Traditional knows how much he has to spend, and buys accordingly—often regardless of which wine he ends up with. A NEO, on the other hand, knows in advance exactly which wine labels he prefers based on quality, taste, region, and variety; and he then goes to Dan Murphy to buy his favourite wines for the best price, often by the case.

In Australia, NEOs are largely metropolitan dwellers, with

more of them living in inner Melbourne and Sydney than anywhere else in Australia. Almost half of all NEOs live in these two urban centres, and are significantly more likely than their Traditional cousins to live in inner Sydney and Melbourne.

Forty-five per cent of NEOs are women and 55 per cent are men; and while NEOs range over all age groups, they tend to be younger than Traditionals. NEOs exceed the national average in every profile between age 20 and age 50, while Traditionals exceed the national average in every profile above age 50.

Half of all Australians with a university degree are NEOs; when compared with Traditionals, four times the number of NEOs have degrees. They are as committed to learning a living as they are to earning a living.

NEOs are most likely to be in professional or management occupations, and earn more than the rest of society. Specifically, they dominate every income category above $45,000 pa, and are five times more likely than anyone else to earn in excess of $100,000 pa. But, remember, they earn more because they are NEOs; they are not NEOs because they earn more.

NEOs also spend more ... and more frequently ... than anyone else. Ninety-one per cent of NEOs are in the top third of discretionary spenders in the Australian economy, compared to only 6 per cent of Traditionals.

Outgoing, gregarious NEOs are great planners, are mobile, and are prepared to take calculated risks. For instance, at any one time 20 per cent of NEOs are actively contemplating a move from their current jobs—compared with 12 per cent of Traditionals. NEOs are also more likely to start and run a small business. This is partly due to their high locus of control (believing success in life is a matter of planning rather than luck) and partly because they are more optimistic about the future than anyone else in the country.

NEOs love the Internet and live much of their life online; this is the place where they can exert individual control and accelerate what we call slow time. The 96 per cent of NEOs who are connected to the Internet like to accelerate slow time by going online to do their banking, share trading, travel bookings, CD and DVD purchasing, and anything else that saves time and helps them jettison mundane tasks.

The Big Swindle

Richard Dawkins, a scientist and the author of *The Selfish Gene,* famously said, 'If something is true, no amount of wishing can make it untrue.' He applauds the ability to reduce extremely complex subjects into simplified forms, to be able to explain that which is otherwise inexplicable in ways that are easily understood—unless, of course, that simplification converts it from the rich and insightful to the simplistic and banal.

Generation why?

Sadly, every day we are assaulted by simplistic and banal reductions of our rich social landscape by the use of terms such as 'baby boomer' and 'generation X' or 'generation Y': crude life-stage descriptors that are favoured by demographers and social commentators hungry for one-size-fits-all solutions to a complex world.

Generations X and Y join the baby boomer label as part of the Big Swindle.

The world is, in Dawkins terms, a more complex place than simple lifestage descriptors can account for, and no amount of wishing by the demographers can make that untrue. Lifestage labels are based on only one factor—age. We all favour simplified concepts, but how can anyone seriously imagine that age could determine our tastes, attitudes, and choices?

Let's take as an example 'generation X'. Gen Xers are all Australians in the 25-to-39 age group. This group necessarily includes priests, alcoholics, politicians, police officers, musicians, unemployed labourers, professors, lovers, haters, lesbians, liberals, believers, heretics, scientologists, CFOs, rich, poor, spenders, savers, technophiles, technophobes ...

In 1991, Canadian writer Douglas Coupland coined the catchphrase 'generation X', and described its members as techno savvy, in control of their lives, and time poor. This is, the story goes, what makes them a force to be reckoned with — a generation to be planned for by governments, and a band of consumers to be attracted and motivated by business. But what about the 34-year-old single mother with three children on welfare trying to find casual work just to pay the bills? She is a gen Xer, and is certainly time poor — but she has no time, money, or energy to learn about new technology, and she lives a life completely out of her control.

It is unarguable that lifestage descriptors provide cues about life-event probabilities aligned with age such as the advent of first-home purchase/mortgage, babies, sea change, downsizing, and retirement. However, what age fails to provide is any insight into why or how choices will be made, or who within the particular age range is most likely to behave one way or the other.

NEOs and Traditionals on either side of the discretionary divide are an example of complex matters made deliciously simple. The 194 factors that define NEOs make them living exemplars of the futility of relying on one factor only. NEOs, for example, are most highly represented in the 25–39 age segment. To a demographer, that would place them squarely in the gen X category. But while NEOs dominate this particular age group, 37 per cent of gen Xers are socially and economically conservative Traditionals. In other words, more than one-third of gen Xers don't like spending money, don't believe they have any influence over their own success, are less educated, and are less interested in learning new things—particularly about technology.

Take another one-factor label: baby boomer (technically defined as anyone born between the end of World War II and the early 1960s). We constantly hear predictions based on the needs of baby boomers as if a 53-year-old academic will behave in ways even vaguely similar to a 57-year-old middle-ranking sales manager in a global corporation. The men live only two suburbs apart in Melbourne, and to a demographer are almost identical. But why should we imagine that these two men would like to read the same books, see the same movies, buy the same motor vehicles, vote for the same political party, believe in the same religious doctrines, and eat the same food?

Society is not homogenous. While age does impose certain common life-stage concerns—such as health, insurance, and so on—behaviours, attitudes, ambitions, tastes, and aspirations will always differ across such a wide range of people. There is strong and reliable evidence that NEO baby boomers, when compared to Traditional baby boomers, will buy completely different health cover and different insurance products, and will approach retirement in vastly different ways.

An American gen Xer declared recently on a global television news service that the Iraq war was not 'their war'; it was George W. Bush's baby-boomer war. The facts do not, however, support this single-factor rhetoric. In the US, 41 per cent of so-called baby boomers vote Democrat, while only 31 per cent vote Republican. Support for the war is limited largely to

Republican voters, and even that support is declining rapidly. So any proposition that the war in Iraq is a baby-boomer war, rather than just a Republican president's war, is pure fantasy. And yet we hear this kind of language every day of the week.

It is unarguable, therefore, that baby boomers do not automatically have anything in common with each other. Nor do they use the same criteria when making lifestyle and spending choices. The new economic order, by contrast, is made up of a band of individuals found across every age group. And it is both their rich complexity and their scientific differentiation from everyone else in society that makes their similarities so identifiable.

ABs pass their use-by date

Australia has been divided by demographers into five socio-economic groups defined by only three basic demographic factors — education, occupation, and income — making them only marginally more useful that the one-factor lifestage descriptors such as generation X. Those in the top socio-economic quintile are known as ABs, and those in the bottom quintile are called FGs.

Traditionals account for four out of five in the bottom FG quintile, while the majority of those in the AB quintile are NEOs. That may appear good news for the use of ABs as a predictor of consumer value. However, the bad news is that one in four are Traditionals. As a consequence, at least a quarter of a company's marketing resources are wasted when directed at ABs as the ideal target market.

In the socially and economically influential media sector, the marketing currency was ABs until NEOs arrived on the scene. For more than twenty years, advertising agencies and marketers viewed and used ABs as the holy grail of high-spending, desirable consumers. Now all that is changing.

Not only do NEOs dominate discretionary spending; they also dominate all *heavy* media consumption. This creates a new consumer currency for marketers and publishers alike. Here is how the differences play out numerically between NEOs and ABs:

Heavy Newspaper Readership (7+ per week)
- 1.5 million NEOs
- 1.4 million ABs

Heavy Magazine Readership (5+ per week)
- 1.8 million NEOs
- 1.3 million ABs

Heavy Commercial Television Viewing (4+ hrs per day)
- 442,000 NEOs
- 260,000 ABs

Heavy Commercial Radio Listening (4+ hrs per day)
- 585,000 NEOs
- 282,000 ABs

Heavy Internet Usage (8+ per week)
- 2.2 million NEOs
- 1.8 million ABs

Heavy Cinema Visitation (2+ visits per quarter)
- 1.9 million NEOs
- 1.3 million ABs

Heavy Addressed-Mail Readership (4+times per week)
- 1.6 million NEOs
- 1.3 million ABs

Heavy 'Out & About' (proxy for outdoor media)
- 1.9 million NEOs
- 1.3 million ABs

Pay-TV Subscribers
- 1.2 million NEOs
- 900,000 ABs

Politics

When it comes to federal politics, the stark political picture is that NEOs are more likely to give their first preferences to the Liberal Party ahead of the Australian Labor Party.

NEOs prefer the coalition because it is, in their view, more likely than the ALP to deliver on economic and business matters. NEOs are, however, 'the new constituency', in that they have well-evolved social and environmental beliefs, and they don't believe the coalition can deliver on those policies as well as the ALP. Additionally, their openness to 'new things' provides an opportunity for all political parties to adopt a reformist agenda. NEOs are deeply influenced by social issues—almost half have progressive social attitudes, while less than one in five has traditional social attitudes. Half of all NEOs are attracted to 'new things', ahead of a third of the population and only a quarter of Traditionals.

Combined, these factors provide an opportunity for the Labor Party to attract NEOs both directly and via preferences from minor parties. To do so in sufficient numbers, however, they will need to establish sound economic and business credentials to complement their social policies. Conversely, the coalition could enhance its attraction to NEOs by boosting its social policies.

Self-Image

Typically, NEOs are outgoing and feel good about themselves, their leisure activities, and their jobs. They like what they do professionally: the majority say they are satisfied by their job, in contrast to one in three Traditionals who feel the same way.

NEOs like to look stylish, and are often extroverted. These individuals think of themselves as 'a bit of an intellectual', believe that success is important, and consider it important to have responsibility in their jobs. NEOs' high locus of control (believing success in life is a matter of planning rather than luck) ensures they are passionate about the Internet, computers, and technology—not because they are early adopters, but rather because new technology gives them more control over their lives.

Sport

NEOs are likely to 'take risks' and to test themselves with intellectual or physical challenges. They are more likely than Traditionals to fly a plane; and, of all the people who compete in triathlons or marathons, NEOs are four times more likely than Traditionals to participate.

Triathlon or marathon competitors are, of course, small in absolute numbers (they comprise only 1 per cent of society). Walking, jogging, and gym work are the most popular exercise activities around the country in absolute terms, with half of all NEOs participating, compared to 40 per cent of Traditionals.

NEOs are a massive four times more likely than Traditionals to participate in snow skiing, 3.3 times more likely to go sailing, three times more likely to scuba dive, 2.4 times more likely to water ski, and twice as likely to go board surfing and body surfing.

The self-reflection and inner-directedness of yoga is particularly attractive to NEOs—they are twice as likely as Traditionals to participate in yoga.

Traditionals are dominant in other sports and leisure activities. They are three times more likely than NEOs to participate in lawn bowls, almost twice as likely to participate in salt water fishing, and one-and-a-half times more likely to hunt and shoot game.

Spectator Sports

Australian Rules is the most popular football code in Australia, with NEOs more than twice as likely to actually attend an AFL match.

Of all the AFL teams in Australia, Sydney Football Club and Melbourne Football Club are, unsurprisingly, the favourite NEO clubs. This is because NEOs live in huge numbers in inner Sydney and Melbourne. It is unsurprising, in the case of Melbourne FC, given that its history is inextricably intertwined with the history of inner Melbourne. It is also unsurprising because the club's management under former newspaper editor Steve Harris had the foresight to marry the activities of the club to other cultural icons, including several in the arts. Remember, NEOs love both AFL and the arts. This is why the AFL club of the future will offer members a wide range of imaginative experiences, only one of which will be attending a football match.

In other codes, NEOs like to watch the Rugby World Cup on television. It's their favourite televised football event, with NEOs 50 per cent more likely than anyone else to watch it on TV.

Entertainment

Entertaining at home is very popular with NEOs. While a quarter of the population hold dinner parties, one in three NEOs cook and entertain at home—in stark contrast to just one in six Traditionals. When it comes to drinking wine, more than half of all NEOs like to drink wine at home, compared to less than a third of Traditionals.

When they do go out, NEOs like to go to the cinema and

to live performances. They are more likely than anyone else to go to the movies, attend live theatre performances, go to the opera or ballet, or attend a music concert. NEOs are even more likely to go to a rock or pop concert; and, while jazz, classical, and blues performances are less popular with them than rock or pop concerts, they are ahead in opera and ballet attendance.

Two-thirds of NEOs over the age of fourteen go to movies in any three-month period, compared to less than half of Traditionals.

In summary, NEOs are passionate, active, involved Australians. In seeking the path less travelled, they still encounter mainstream culture (such as football), but it is their individual twist on the mainstream that distinguishes them.

-3-

Making Social Waves

When Arthur C Clarke wrote of a new world and Stanley Kubrick depicted it on the big screen in *2001: A Space Odyssey*, we imagined a new millennium in which evolution was all but complete, if such a thing were possible. This would be a place where the lowly primate had fully evolved into a computer-assisted interplanetary traveller conquering all horizons and the challenges of space and time.

Six years earlier, Marshall McLuhan had predicted the emergence of the 'global village', writing compellingly of the leapfrog improvements in society, particularly the immense social leap propelled by the new literacy, which was in turn brought about by the invention of the printing press.

In the years since the prophetic 1960s, much has changed. McLuhan's global village has become a reality, and the computer and the Internet have vastly outdone the printing press as stimulants of social change.

Clarke's evolved world has also arrived, but not quite in the way he predicted. Outer space is not the final frontier awaiting exploration by evolved beings. Rather, the inner space of the mind and body has emerged as the shape of the new frontier. And the 'final frontier' may be even smaller as we explore the atomic world of quantum mechanics and its application to atomic-sized and sub-atomic-sized computers. We are welcoming a world in which the very building blocks of matter are combining to form a computer so minuscule it cannot be seen, but so powerful it will out-process the largest computer on earth.

As these frontiers move from massive to miniscule, the same shift is happening in society.

We are moving from the unquestioned influence of the giant to the unstoppable momentum of the individual. Clarke got the future right in principle; he was just askew on scale. We do lead computer-assisted lives, but only one in four of us—the NEOs—recognise the Information Age as the perfect vehicle for assuming small pieces of individual power and influence. And, while members of the new economic order embrace the employment, mobility, and communications benefits of globalisation, they abhor the institutionalised power that globalisation delivers to the shrinking number of expanding governments and corporations. If this seems paradoxical, you have just gained your first insight into the intricate psyche of a NEO.

Marshall McLuhan declared that the medium was the message. Microsoft founder Bill Gates painted the information superhighway as the pathway to the future. And Arthur C Clarke depicted our future as a techno-world in which the computer not only enjoyed superhuman intelligence but also exhibited the wisdom of Solomon.

It is true that we have enjoyed breathtaking advances in technology, although none of them seem to have delivered the time-savings our parents and grandparents imagined in the 1950s and 1960s. The changes have been extraordinary nonetheless, and the improvements in communications unimaginable—even by McLuhan's and Clarke's standards. But it is not technology that has created the new world.

What we are experiencing through NEOs is individual determinism rather than technological determinism. The post-industrial Information Age has certainly changed what we can do, but it has not changed what we want to do.

The globalised world is abuzz with talk of economies—the old economy and the new economy. We are bombarded with the latest news of the NASDAQ's rise and fall, or the performance of the Euro against the US dollar. Globalisation has made real the old truism that when the USA sneezes the rest of the world catches cold. But world economies are manifestations of world societies—not the other way around. We are not experiencing economic determinism any more than we are being led by technology.

So what is shaping the new world, if it is not the Information Age or the world of the new economy?

The world is increasingly a place where a revolutionary kind of dynamic exists, with NEOs and Traditionals expecting totally different treatment and experiences. While we all feel its impact and even see its symptoms, until now we have been unable to identify its cause.

The Third Wave

Modern history can be broken into a number of waves, each capturing a major social and economic movement. The First Wave covers the period from the agrarian age through to the Industrial Revolution, and is characterised by a hand-to-mouth existence. It was an age when people produced what they needed, when they needed it.

The Second Wave runs from the early twentieth century through to the early twenty-first century, and represents the era of mass production and mass marketing. It is the one-size-fits-all industrial or modernist age.

The Third Wave is the post-industrial Information Age.

the Second Wave and Third Wave co-exist, just as
als and NEOs co-exist. But in the same way that
als and NEOs are fundamentally different so, too,
the Second and Third Waves are as different as flour and
croissants.

The Second Wave is a useful metaphor for a society that
still values a globalised world of big government and bigger
corporations. This is the modernist world of universal rules
for the majority. While we have been riding the crest of the
Second Wave and enjoying its bounty, it has peaked.

The Third Wave, on the other hand, is emerging from its
nascent stage.

Old habits die hard, however. The Second Wave passion
for a simple solution lingers. The historically seductive notions
of central authority, mass production, and mass marketing
pervade most traditional institutions. These range from
corporations to political parties and local government
authorities; from global banks to international retailers; and
from global media organisations to the very automobile
manufacturers that pioneered the universal production
model. Think of Henry Ford pumping identical cars off the
first automobile production line, inviting consumers to have
a new car in any colour they liked … as long as it was black.

What better example could we find of the mindset, 'We
will produce what we do best and most efficiently and then
we'll sell it to a grateful (homogeneous) world'? As Traditional
companies produce more and more in an attempt to compete
for consumers' attention, they are paradoxically shifting
control to the consumer. More competition equals more
power for people in the street.

In this scramble for attention, manufacturers create new
and improved products, making immediately obsolete the
one just purchased. In one business-as-usual year, UK bank

NatWest introduced 240 new or improved products. Telecommunications companies routinely maintain portfolios of thousands of 'products' (complex product, service, and pricing combinations) that are perceived as necessary to attract customer attention in a crowded marketplace of competing suppliers.

What this production explosion/supply model fails to recognise is that most consumers — not just NEOs — only want those products, services, and experiences that are *meaningful* to them *personally*, rather than those that the corporations would like to produce. It also fails to take into account the fact that, as demonstrated repeatedly in psychological tests, more than six choices or product options cause cognitive overload in consumers. Not only do consumers get increasingly fatigued and confused; there is an inverse relationship between the number of choices offered and a consumer's likelihood to make a purchase.

So, in the Second Wave, where we find the mass production/mass marketing model, we also find more mass consumer choice. And the Internet is showing consumers how to narrow their choices in satisfying their individual needs.

Even a general portal such as Yahoo.com, which can also be tailored to suit personal layout preferences, will provide stock price information sorted according to personal preferences. It will send us a reminder of a friend's birthday and then, in a single online transaction, choose a present with our choice of gift-wrapping and birthday card with our personalised greeting, all with the support of a customer-service agent on the telephone if we need it. The speed, ease, and immediacy of satisfying these choices are almost impossible to experience in the physical world. Yet, precisely because they are available online, we expect them to also be offered by their physical offline counterparts.

The Internet: the engine of change

It comes as no surprise that the Internet is the engine of the Third Wave and the space of choice for NEOs. On the Internet, NEOs can be themselves and can control their own universe. It is the mind space most comfortable and attractive to NEOs because it is the place where they are able to be whomever and whatever they have an appetite to be. The control that NEOs achieve over their own lives through the Internet is in stark contrast to a corporation or authority trying to impose its values on an individual.

Accordingly, the future of the Internet will have less to do with the improvements we can make to technology and much more to do with how it can energise NEOs to discover and conquer new frontiers.

The Third Wave world of the Internet is, however, a complex place where success is not guaranteed.

During 1999 there were 457 IPOs, or stockmarket floats, in the US—117 of which experienced a doubling of their opening price on the first day of trading. Dot-com floats were happening daily, and speculators were bullish as the new millennium dawned.

Then, on 11 March 2000, the dot-com boom turned into the tech-wreck. The continued denial of heady unreality was suddenly unmasked. One wise observer quipped that when speed and greed become the creed, you bleed. What happened in 2000 was more like a haemorrhage.

Over the next two years, the NASDAQ lost 78 per cent of its value, falling from 5047 points to 1114.

In Australia, the impact was just as dramatic. The share price of that darling of the stock exchange, Melbourne IT, fell to just 74 cents from its stellar heights of $16.37.

Today, with the tech-wreck still a living memory, all seems to be forgiven. Less than five years after the official end of the dot-com crash, technology stocks are back in fashion. Only this time, the attraction is based on results rather than rumour.

In 2005, Melbourne IT announced an 82 per cent lift in profit for the full year, and in 2006 its share price returned to a respectable $1.70, outperforming both the S&P and the ASX200. Admittedly, it was not back to the heady heights of the boom, but its price reflected the return to favour of the tech stocks.

And is it any wonder the online world is back in favour with investors? While the venture capitalists were licking their wounds and decrying the online industry as a disaster, consumers around the world were licking their lips as they used the Internet to enrich their lives.

Since 2000, the Internet has been the only media channel to experience an increase in consumer usage. Television, magazines, newspapers, and cinema are all flat, with radio suffering a downturn. Not only have traditional media failed to achieve any growth, but the explosion in Internet usage has resulted in a decline in traditional media

A surprising 20 per cent of consumers who use the Internet at least once a month also watch less television than they used to. Around one in ten read fewer newspapers and magazines, and listen less to radio. In the US, time spent consuming the Internet has reached the same level as the time spent reading a newspaper.

This is important for the advertising industry, which is often considered the barometer of the health of the economy.

In the US and the UK, online advertising has reached around 4 per cent of the total amount spent on advertising. This figure is significant for two reasons. The first is that, at this level in the UK, it now outstrips spending on radio advertising; the second is that online spending is now more than four times greater than it was at the height of the dot-com boom in 2000.

In Australia, online advertising has attracted more than 6 per cent of all media spending. It has already overtaken cinema, pay TV, and outdoor advertising, and is set to pass consumer magazines.

The online market is back in business, and is looking stronger than ever. Those service providers that failed in the infant online market did so either because they had a bad business idea or a poor business model. Just as technology cannot be seen as the saviour of business, it conversely can't be seen as the destroyer.

One common weakness characterises those businesses still facing extinction—they don't know *who* they're in business for. They have no idea who is going to reward them with large and frequent high-margin orders. They fail to see the two different journeys required for the two different economic streams in the Third Wave.

The success stories, on the other hand, are those enterprises that know they are in business for either NEOs or Traditionals. And if they are in business for both, they know they must design completely different products, services, experiences, communications, management styles, and cultures for each type.

Most traditional bricks-and-mortar corporations have developed online strategies as an additional channel—becoming what is known as multi-channel players. They link a website to their bricks-and-mortar operation and replicate what they do in the traditional economy.

This is particularly applicable in the retail sector. A multi-channel retailer's higher gross margins, cost-efficient logistics, and lower marketing costs make good economic sense, enabling them to compete fiercely with the Internet-only, or pure-play, enterprises. This multi-channel model has enabled the giant US book retailer Barnes & Noble to be the only serious Internet competitor to the pure-play Amazon.com.

But, for all their Internet effort, neither Barnes & Noble nor Amazon has recognised the opportunity to create a totally different experience for the two different types of consumer—one high-relationship and high-margin, the other low-aspiration and low-margin. By failing to differentiate between the two types of customer, each company is incurring the same costs for both high-value and low-value customers, and less than optimum margin from the high-value customers.

For example, NEOs buy more than twice as many books as Traditionals, and don't expect an automatic discount. This impacts two of the major determinants of profitability on the Net—order size and margin. If an online bookseller can double its order size and increase its margin (by not giving it away as unnecessary discounts), its probability of profitability and success soar. And almost all NEOs are online every day.

According to a McKinsey & Company survey, only 8 per cent of Internet shoppers are searching for a discount; and 80 per cent of book shoppers typically visit only one site, and usually not the one with the lowest prices.

Another key characteristic of the Third Wave is velocity—particularly, the concept of fast time. It took decades for a bricks-and-mortar, traditional-economy or Second Wave business to create any sense of market dominance—growth characterised by inflexibility and slow time. Now, at the beginning of the Third Wave, it takes years, not decades, and soon will only take months.

Consider Dr Harry Nudel in New York City. Harry very successfully sells hard-to-find and out-of-print art books online. But does this bookseller, recently the darling of venture capitalists, own a chain of traditional bricks-and-mortar stores? No way! Harry's operation is so flexible that he sells his books around the world in fast time online. And, as for flexibility, if you want to touch and feel in slow time the books that Harry sells and to have a little personal engagement with him, you'll find him selling books from the boot of his car on Prince Street in SoHo—or will that be Mercer Street today? Third Wave Harry is a NEO's NEO.

Third Wave technology is, however, just ... technology. It simply enables. Without a clear business strategy it enables nothing.

Post-Everything

Modernism meant rules and structure. Postmodernism meant an artificial anarchic free for all. NEO-Modernism cherishes freedom and imagination, but places it in a framework of ordered intelligence. This is the new order, and the new order will eventually lead society into a post-linear world in which stories are told only through the screen.

According to eminent scientist Susan Greenfield:

> Outside of formal education, future toys, like everything else, will be highly interactive: so the growing child will see the outside world as inconstant and malleable. Our successors will increasingly be 'people of the screen' compared to the 20th century 'people of the book'. There will no longer be a need to read or write, thanks to voice-activated computers and the trend towards icon manipulation and instant access. Inevitably, therefore, there will be changes not just in literacy skills but also those of the imagination. The future generations will think differently: although they will have a much narrower attention span, it will be coupled with a transcendence of time and space.

They will be able to imagine and be creative, free from the strictures of a linear culture, and simultaneously free from the need to demonstrate that post-modern appearance of forced liberation.

Waving Goodbye

When, in twenty or thirty years, sociologists and historians reflect on the beginning of the twenty-first century, they will marvel at the velocity of change and the intensity of the power in the Third Wave.

They will observe the international boom of the late-twentieth and early twenty-first centuries, and see in it what many institutions failed to do. They will recognise the late Second Wave boom as a paradox—a time in which success inertia was the very reason corporations failed to change, and so planted the seeds of their own failure.

Historians will ponder about how so many diverse strands and influences converged and then, at the end of the twentieth century, formed a new wave to sweep the world. Economists, on the other hand, will marvel at how business failed to see the Third Wave and the gap that existed between the Second and Third Waves; and how the failure of business to understand its implications for the world economy brought the boom to an end.

We have begun surfing the Third Wave; but NEOs are already there, paddling like mad.

NEOS in the Third Space

NEOs play, work, and live in new and interesting ways. Nothing is predictable. A unique leisure experience may be so attractive to NEOs that they will shower it with discretionary dollars. Or an employer may be seeking new insights on how to attract NEOs to the workforce, and how to keep them challenged and happily productive. A landlord may even want to sell NEOs a house, or furnish an apartment, or rent them a sea-change getaway at some exotic beach.

The Third Place

American sociologist Ray Oldenburg wrote of the Third Place in his book *The Great Good Place*. His Third Place is that important physical space in our lives beyond work and the home; for example, the place that existed in rural life or in a medieval town, but has been lost in the transition to our modern lives, cities, and societies.

Oldenburg observes that we have become obsessed and consumed by work. In doing so we have lost the 'other' place where we used to create communities. Indeed, we have lost our very sense of community. The neighbourhood of our childhood was the place we played, where we had fun, where many of our formative experiences were incubated.

With the commercial momentum of the traditional economy, that neighbourhood changed as corporations encroached on the places of childhood memory. Shopping malls were developed on the open fields where people used to picnic. Picnickers became customers. Neighbourhood sports fields became stadiums, and watching a game suddenly came with an admission price.

Competition for what became known as the 'leisure dollar' fuelled these vast sporting facilities, titanic shopping malls and all-pervasive television programs. The TV programmers controlled when we could dip into our electronic Third Place and what we would find when we got there. Corporations controlled what was on the radio and what was in the newspapers. Individuals had no capability, nor any conscious desire, to exert influence over the experiences that filled the vacuum created by the absence of a Third Place.

When the football match was at the corner oval it was owned by the community but had no commercial value and therefore had no place in the traditional economy. It had to be commercialised. Accordingly, the corporations that set the rules in the traditional economy moved to own the culture that satisfied the need for 'some place else' in the community.

Today, large corporations own international sport, be it tennis and golf around the world, football, baseball and basketball in the US, soccer and cricket in the UK, and even the Olympics and its global influence. And that's fine with Traditionals because it fills their vacuum, their slow time. It provides a release, a spectacle, competition and challenge, and some sense of affiliation even if they can exert no real influence over it.

The original owner of US baseball's Boston Red Sox, John Taylor, built a ballpark in amongst residential estates he already owned. Years later, successive owners and managers have consciously developed Fenway Park (rather than the team or its individual players) into a strong brand, profiting from an understanding of customers' need for a place that provided strong local identification and a means of bonding with people who shared a common experience of losing. The Red Sox, as a team, have played well but rarely won, and yet they enjoy consistent profits from high-capacity crowds and record levels of pre-game sales. Fenway Park is an example of a Third Place.

The need for the Third Place can be attributed to our loss of individual identity in the traditional economy, and to a longing for what could not be found in either the workplace or the home.

NEOs, however, are online. On the Web they are satisfying their immediate needs for community and are redefining the various leisure roles and recreational activities that complete their personal picture and fulfil their lives.

The Third Place, in Oldenburg's sense, becomes less relevant in the NEO economy because of the convergence of new technology into their homes, workplaces, and community spaces. What dominates is the space that NEOs control, where they can explore and celebrate their individuality—a place that isn't 'owned' by corporations. Most frequently, this *place* is the online universe.

As a society we know where our *work* takes place and how it has evolved. We know the role that *home* plays in our social fabric and how it has evolved. We all understand what we mean when we talk about these places. But we haven't yet found a common language or understanding of the space that exists outside home and work, a space that truly defines who we are as members of our tribes and communities and as members of broader society.

Oldenburg's Third Place was useful in the twentieth century. But NEOs are rewriting the rules about community and leisure, just as they are rewriting the rules for *home* and *work*.

The Third Space

So how do NEOs describe the new leisure space that combines the Internet with the local park? What is their version of the Third Place?

The answer is the Third Space.

The Third Space encompasses the leisure experiences NEOs desire, and it celebrates them in both the actual and virtual world. The Third Space creates a personal culture, where NEOs find excitement and challenge, and where they explore books, music, food, travel; myriad creative experiences that uplift their spirits and form intense communities. In the Third Space, NEOs find and create their own space, anywhere in the world, and populate it with people who stimulate their personal discovery. And they don't care if it's in the physical world or online.

Combining the cultural and leisure passions that sit at the very heart of the NEO psyche, the Third Space, while not automatically a physical place, has an undeniable sense of place. It embodies the spirit of discovery, exploration, and escape. It offers culture that is applied or implied, physical or abstract.

The Third Space is the space of knowledge and the mind. It is where NEOs challenge themselves creatively and intellectually in everyday life and through the parallel universe of the digital world. But because NEOs value high-touch or high-involvement activities, as well as hi-tech ones, they also explore the physical Third Space through literature, art, food, wine, and the beauty of the eucalypt or the salt of the sea.

In the Third Space they could be online, at home, in a bar or a bookstore, or simply with other people just like them. NEOs will congregate wherever they find other NEOs. And when they formalise the relationships between living spaces, thinking spaces and playing spaces, they create the new village or NEO neighbourhood.

For example, it is not necessarily the physical elements of Greenwich Village in New York City that make it attractive to NEOs. It is its cultural pluralism, creativity, and diverse community spirit that makes it a Third Space where NEOs think, drink, and live on the brink.

For NEOs the Third Space is a place to escape to and a journey of self-discovery. And because they're 24/7 people, it is explored at any time of the day or night.

Recognising this fact, game publisher Electronic Arts developed a game specifically designed for adults for whom work, home, and the community blur into one 24/7 smorgasbord. 'Majestic' is an online mystery game where the clues are delivered via mobile phone, email, pager, or website. In the middle of a business meeting, on a trip to the supermarket, or simply while updating the day's schedule on the bus on the way to work, your phone vibrates or you receive an email with a clue. The clues may be the sound of a bloodcurdling scream, or may be an imaginary shadowy underworld figure leaving you instructions for your next session online. Such games stimulate the imagination and provide a sense of intrigue that heightens the experience of everyday life.

However, the Third Space is more than just an escape to a place beyond work and home and the world of transactions. It's the space in which NEOs celebrate who they are and what they stand for. It's the space, whether actual or virtual, in which they are allowed to be all the people they wish to be and to discover all the other worlds they wish to discover.

The Third Space is not obvious to everyone. It is c a coded passkey or secret handshake, a whispered s˅ known only to NEOs. For example, a NEO walking down a dark Melbourne lane reads the imperceptible, coded signs that alert them to a great bar which, to the casual Traditional observer, is totally invisible. Not only do these *invisible* bars have no signage, but when a thirsty drinker calls directory assistance for a phone number they discover the bar is unlisted. NEOs are comfortable with 'no-brands', because their Third Space stands for complexity and sophistication rather than the transactional and observable.

This phenomenon of codified experience is not exclusive to darkened lanes in Melbourne. A case in point is a busy bar in a decidedly unfashionable part of Manhattan's West Village. An insignificant sign reading Employees Only sits atop an old double fronted shop with a fortune-teller in the window lit only by a flickering neon sign announcing 'Psychic', which is precisely what you would need to be to recognise this as one of New York's hottest cocktail bar restaurants.

The Third Space is therefore not characterised by the big noise or the obvious sign and has nothing to do with traditional advertising and promotions.

In the Third Space, consumers have to *feel* individual. It must deliver authenticity and be edgy. Fundamentally, to qualify as the new leisure space, it has to be invisible, or at least inaccessible or confusing to Traditionals, and NEOs have to be in control.

Consider movies and sporting events. As Oldenburg observes, corporations decide what we see and where and when we see it.

Entertainment organisations in the USA are already feeling the effects of this growing demand for personalisation. More than 25 per cent of Americans watch videos on their computer every week and more than half have used a computer to download and listen to music. The iPod era is a fixture.

Unfortunately for cinema operators, while the number of US cinema screens grew by 62 per cent between 1998 and 2001, ticket sales increased by only 16 per cent.

In Australia, heavy cinema visitation (two visits in 3 months) dropped 2 per cent to 29 per cent between 2000 and 2005. NEOs have always seen more movies than anyone else and after hitting a high in 2002 of 49 per cent, they slipped to 47 per cent in 2005. This is in stark contrast to their heavy Internet use (8 or more times a week), which jumped from 28 per cent in 2000 to 54 per cent in 2005.

When it comes to Australian free-to-air television and to a lesser extent subscription TV, NEOs accustomed to getting what they want when they want it, are seeing a bloated, out-dated model with out-of-touch executives scheduling movies at times that suit the channels and advertisers, not the viewers. And the programmers are drawing from a limited library of titles that don't reflect the rapidly evolving demand for new content.

In the Third Space, however, NEOs decide what they will see with movies-on-demand and TiVo to find and digitally record only the television programs they want from anywhere on the planet. They decide what is right for them, choose it and then participate in it. Yahoo! Inc. has already announced that users of its TV-listings Web page will be able to record to a TiVo device at the click of a button. They can listen to radio and music programmes that exactly match their new or abiding interests by downloading them to their iPod and lis-tening to them in their own time, in their own space.

The Third Space Rules

It is apparent from all the evidence that Traditional economic principles have no place in the NEO economy. For example, the institutional logos that act as symbols of solid-state corporate certainty in the traditional economy have no place in the Third Space.

Enterprises need not go to the extreme of the secret bar in the mysterious Melbourne laneway or the coded invisibility of Employees Only in New York's West Village. Nor do they necessarily need to go to the no-logo extreme, although for some it is the perfect solution.

A successful symbol in the Third Space is one that stands for the values and beliefs of NEOs rather than the brand essence of a corporation. The iPod is a good example: it communicates beauty and design by using people whose faces we never see.

The market abounds with competitors to Apple's iPod, so why has this music player not only made MP3 the standard music-transfer format, but also, in outselling every other player on the market, transformed MP3 players into the hottest category in the consumer electronics market?

The iPod has become a symbol of individual choice; after all, we make our iPod what we want it to be by choosing the music we want and listening to it when it suits us. And the ambiguous silhouette figures in the marketing campaign allow us to put ourselves in the picture in our very own personal space.

The iPod has become a tertiary symbol of NEO values and aspirations—way beyond the functions and features of the player itself. The other MP3 players on the market are just examples of very good consumer technology.

The Third Space is the place where iPods surface with their symbolism firmly in the hands of NEOs rather than a corporation. Yes, there is a powerful corporation behind the millions of iPods sold, but it is a corporation with a human face, a deconstructed values set, and a long-term commitment to making beautiful sculptural objects that, in keeping their practical utility, also convert into signs or symbols of meaning. In the Third Space, products such as Apple's iPod are transformed into symbols that convey messages, not just about themselves but also about the people who value them, the people who consume them. They are NEO symbols of desire.

The Third Space is therefore principally a place of symbolism and meaning: online or offline. It isn't where we reside and live. It isn't where we produce and work. It's where we escape from rules to discover those experiences that give meaning to our lives. It's www.snowgoose.com.au, it's www.williams-sonoma.com, it's James Street in Brisbane's Fortitude Valley, it's the aquamarine water at the Friendly Beaches in Tasmania's East coast, it's Cradle Mountain, it's the Yamba prawn pasta at Sydney's Bambini Trust restaurant, it's the truffle pizza at the Mercer Kitchen in New York, it's anything Horuki Murakami or Tim Winton care to write, it's Brian Eno. It's sights, sounds, tastes, flavours, sensations. It's luscious, sometimes luxurious, always sensory, and always brimming with symbolism of a life left somehow poorer without these experiences. Sometimes it's where and how we shop. Sometimes it's nothing to do with transactions at all. But it's always that thing we do that fills our souls with pleasure, beyond the strictures of home and work.

There's no easy way to decode the Third Space into neat, modular, supply-chain elements because not everything outside the experiences of home and work are automatically NEO elements of the Third Space. Any product or experience needs to earn its place at the sensory crossroads.

US coffee chain Starbucks and bookseller Borders, offering leisure and recreation, are not part of the Third Space because, for NEOs, they are far too contrived, can be decoded too quickly, and lack the quality of authenticity. Instead, NEOs must be free to explore for themselves, personalise the experience, and imbue the brand with their own values and beliefs.

Those, however, who deliver the right Third Space experience to NEOs will be rewarded with a valuable relationship and abiding loyalty.

Every great city has a shop that has been selling ground coffee, pastries, Italian groceries, or fresh pasta for the past thirty years without changing. These experiences are being rediscovered by NEOs who love experiences that offer authenticity and personalisation. The transaction, while central to the relationship, is secondary to the experience and personal meaning.

The sense of theatre, the noise, the personal recognition and engagement all make the experiences memorable. NEOs cherish the corner store that survived the onslaught of the supermarket and the shopping mall. They celebrate its historic authenticity. But if these authentic enterprises can also introduce a twenty-first century experience and develop a fresh focus on delivering individual experiences, they transform their heritage into the NEO economy and create an authentic role in the Third Space.

NEOs tend to buy quirky second-hand European cars that would traditionally have been categorised as an expression of the owner's personality. But, it is much more than that. The eccentric European car becomes just one element of a whole new way of life for NEOs. The car becomes part of the NEOs' Third Space and symbolises what they stand for.

Extending the automotive example a step further, if the

specialist mechanic who services the much-loved European car treats it as a tertiary symbol rather than just another piece of machinery, he shifts from the traditional economy into the NEO economy and enjoys the financial benefit that comes with staking a place in the Third Space. By loving and cherishing the car, the mechanic also treats its owner as an individual. The mechanic creates a personal engagement with the (premium) transaction in the background.

As another example, the owner of the terminally hip bar in Melbourne laneway might change its format every six months, either by changing locations or alternatively changing the feel of the place from a seedy gin palace with old-fashioned overhead fans to a hard-edged martini bar.

As a consequence of this constant evolution and change, when a NEO and her friends go out for drinks, while remaining loyal to their favourite nightspots, they keep discovering new experiences. They don't need to chop and change because the venues they visit reinvent themselves, providing the NEO and her friends with the challenge of constantly changing experiences.

This is not a challenge welcomed by a Traditional and his friends, however. They spend every Friday night in a themed Irish pub attracted by the 'happy hour' with cut-price drinks between 5.30 p.m. and 7.00 p.m. They value the comfort of knowing exactly what to expect on their regular outing.

By engaging the Third Space, NEOs can live and work in smaller physical spaces because they have access to, and are in control of, their *other* lives. Both in the physical world and the online world the Third Space is larger because it provides rich and constantly changing experiences for them to enjoy.

Alternatively, NEOs can trade smaller workspaces for larger personal spaces at home. They can make a sea change to a larger home space in the country or at the beach because technology makes it possible to trade office space with home space. If they do make a sea-change decision they need less office space but more virtual Third Space, because they're more isolated and have fewer opportunities to engage face-to-face than they did when they worked in an office every day of the week.

NEOs also carry the Third Space with them. The concept of a nightclub in one fixed spot is irrelevant when in every world city there are scores of NEO experiences, each one in a new location with a new offering.

NEOs in Sweden have the benefit of the Third Space working for them at all times. They have the help of a dating service that calls their mobile phone when they are in physical proximity with someone who shares their interests and aspirations. The service calls the other person at the same time, so the two parties can meet if they so desire.

Anywhere, anytime, NEOs connect with people like themselves in the Third Space.

-5-
NEOs at Work

The nature of work is changing, and the relationship between employer and employee is changing from hierarchy to equality. NEOs view work not as a separate and distinct activity that happens between the hours of nine and five but, rather, as an extension of their lives. For NEOs, work has little to do with time-keeping, and the separation between work and leisure is increasingly blurred.

NEOs are not workaholics—they are lifeaholics. They define themselves not by their work but by their interests, talents, and abilities.

Who happens to pay for those talents is less important than the talents themselves. And there will be many things NEOs do that they will not get paid for. For example, a NEO may be a well-paid stockmarket analyst in a large broking house, as well as being an author or composer or an expert gardener. A NEO may be a business analyst in an energy company by day, while also splitting 'spare' time between a voluntary position on the executive of a national homeless youth initiative and earning money writing occasional articles for a business magazine.

What a Traditional does for a living, on the other hand, defines who he is. A Traditional might be a teacher who, in every passage of a busy life, thinks of himself as just that. He also gets involved in extra-curricular activities, but they all relate to his role in life as a teacher.

If our business analyst NEO lost her job, she would move quickly into a similar role in another corporation; and if there were no comparable jobs available she would turn immediately to a completely different career-path in journalism or the not-for-profit sector. The Traditional teacher, on the other hand, would be lost and bereft if he lost his job and couldn't get another one as a teacher. He is a teacher first and an individual second. He would not even know where to begin a career beyond teaching.

To NEOs, financial reward is a measure of their employer's regard for their talents and contribution. If it doesn't parallel their self-worth, they simply change jobs.

But the work that NEOs do is never regarded as 'just a job' or as a place to fill in time. No matter how much balance they promise themselves and no matter how many promises they make to finish work at a reasonable hour, responsibility always gets in the way. They can never escape the deep sense of accountability and commitment they feel.

They do, however, insist on a new way of working in return for this deep dedication. The conventional workplace with a traditional authority-structure is less and less popular with NEOs.

Anyone who offers NEOs a traditional workplace runs the risk of losing valuable employees. NEOs need a workplace culture that recognises and manages talent and imagination; while this might appear difficult for a large institution to undertake, it is absolutely essential.

A NEO enterprise doesn't need large numbers of employees. Instead, it will probably have alliances with individuals and other businesses where communities are formed and re-formed around interesting and challenging projects. The IT sector already operates in this way, with specialists hired for their individual skills and experience to work on short-term projects.

In the immediate future, NEO enterprises will have fewer and fewer employees and a series of outsourced human resources who, in turn, will supervise or hire other subcontractors. High-aspiration, highly committed NEOs have completely different expectations to their Traditional colleagues.

NEOs are free to move unshackled by the traditional anchors. Smart employers have established frameworks that allow NEOs to move not only within that company but across the city, across other businesses, and across the world. For NEOs, it's not enough to develop a tried-and-true range of skills; they need to find new frontiers and challenges.

Organisations that fail to recognise and deliver new challenges will fail to keep NEOs. That said, large corporations often feel that NEOs are trying to acquire power in order to appropriate control. This fundamentally fails to understand what drives NEOs. They want personal power and influence, but they do not want the power of the corporation. NEOs don't necessarily want power over others. They do, however, want to control their own futures.

Work Attractive to NEOs

NEOs will certainly be attracted to knowledge jobs because they involve the decoding of complexity. A job that values change, provides a challenge, and offers freedom to move will be attractive to NEOs. This implies a role that requires imagination, creativity, and a sense of innovation and leadership—so it rules out the bank clerk, the cost accountant, and the conveyancing lawyer. It rules out the repetitive, and probably even rules out a person working on his or her own, unless it is in a particularly creative and challenging role.

NEOs will look 'under the cover' of any new job to examine its potential because the true nature of the position may have been masked by a corporate job-description emphasising structure and productivity. For example, a NEO may be one of the new breed of project managers who, although they are not the best managers of individual tasks, are capable of decoding complexity and creative problem-solving, and thrive on personal challenge. This is different from a more traditional project manager who, given a project plan with milestones and budgets, can execute tasks and manage resources, but who may not be good at managing either complexity or the unexpected.

Designing new systems, looking at how the world could be different, pushing the envelope of what is possible with technology; this type of work responds to the appetite of NEOs for a personal challenge at the very edge of convention.

NEOs typically are intelligent, very well educated, mobile, creative, and talented. Traditional organisations find it difficult to manage these characteristics. To retain employees such as this, however, they will have to learn how to recognise and manage the qualities of NEOs that have the potential to add the greatest value and differentiation to their organisations.

Rewards for NEOs

One way to recognise and retain NEOs is to pay them well. Because they practise continuous high-value consumption, they need money. NEOs are ambitious, but not in a traditional way. They aspire to experiences that are better than they are currently having. Money is important, so they need to have significant rewards. NEOs are expensive. And they're worth it.

Money, while critically important as fuel for the ambitions of NEOs, is also a measure of an employer's regard. But it is only one measure.

They yearn for the freedom to exert personal views, thoughts, opinions, and the full range of their intelligence to positively influence outcomes. Recognition of the influence NEOs have and the contribution they make is a reward in itself.

Challenges for NEOs

NEOs constantly want to be put to the test. They are intellectually and emotionally free to move, so if they are not challenged they'll find a new organisation, or a new team, or a new task that offers more stimulation.

To retain the valuable talent of a NEO, managers need to provide a collegial environment involving other people like them, either by surrounding or connecting them with their colleagues. Engagement is critical, and it doesn't necessarily have to be with people inside the organisation they work for. There are circles of intent and interest that operate across organisations in which NEOs network comfortably and competently, and find real satisfaction. To fail to provide a rich, challenging, and collegial environment is to provide temptation for valuable NEOs to graze across other organisations in search of other soul mates. And who knows? They might just find the pastures a little greener in those other organisations.

This is a big shift to consider. There are myriad issues such as privacy and confidentiality to be addressed in the creation of an open environment. These are issues that must, however, be addressed because NEOs define themselves by their engagement and connection with others in producing a constant flow of fresh ideas and thinking.

One model of this type of cross-organisational work team is found in the elite world of medical research, where specialists from across the world, across disciplines and across skill sets, form a community that stands for something new and challenging. Good examples include the teams involved in the human genome project, AIDS cure research, and the search for a cure for breast cancer.

The NEO Workplace

A NEO workplace has the look and feel of an environment designed, not for the organisation, but for the people who work there. It is designed around the people who use it, and the interface between customer and employee is a tissue rather than a wall. This organic, user-based connectivity celebrates the knowledge–work nature of most NEO enterprises.

How NEOs do their work depends on how the workplace itself has been structured. It isn't enough that a workplace has an iconic staff 'canteen' designed by a renowned international architect if the rest of the workplace is designed in the traditional mode. The building and its facilities must all be designed to assist people to work in high-performance teams operating in a 24/7 world, free to reconfigure their facilities to fit their work objectives. Factor-in a place to live, and a range of cultural activities, and the workplace is being redefined as one suited to NEOs.

NEOs are less and less interested in coming to work at all. They don't make the distinction between work and other activities because their brains are always engaged. The experience is important; they seek experience as well as achievement, but don't want achievement at the expense of experience. A common comment from NEOs about jobs they have left is, 'The money was great but I was bored out of my brain.'

A NEO workplace will be need to be restructured to provide NEOs with a flexible, changing set of experiences and facilities that match the work they are engaged in. And a NEO is just the person to help restructure a workplace because she doesn't need the certainty of a physical structure. This is made obvious when observing, close to large office buildings, the coffee bars and restaurants full of people doing real work.

But why aren't they doing it in their office space? What does this tell us?

Traditional managers worry about productivity levels because everyone keeps going out to have coffee. While this concern may be appropriate for Traditionals, NEOs are busy having collegial relationships that are central to productive work.

The emergent NEO workplace sometimes resembles a university campus because it has human-scale buildings housing many disciplines in one location, along with support facilities such as libraries, coffee bars, and gyms. This university-campus model is only apposite when it's not the infrastructure that's important; it's how people relate to it that matters.

The NEO workplace is a 'thinking colosseum' where people come to test their own ideas, principles, and theories in a robust and challenging environment filled with colleagues. In this model there is a menu of learning activities including lectures, tutorials, and assignments. There are also clear performance-objectives that people work to achieve, either together or separately. If a NEO advances to another level in a year's time it's not because he put in the hours; it's because of what he achieved in thought leadership or project management.

Most organisations are, however, slow to change.

Traditional corporations have responded to the fact that 57 per cent of online banking and shopping is done at work by establishing rules to restrict personal access to the Internet, seeing it as a waste of the corporation's time and a cause of lower productivity.

NEO enterprise managers, on the other hand, understand that because their employees are 24/7 people, they are using technology to accelerate slow time. Ordering online frees up time later in the day that would otherwise be required for travel to bricks-and-mortar banks and retailers, with their time-wasting queues.

NEOs switch slow time and fast time to their advantage to make the most of their own productivity. This rewards employers with, rather than robs them of, employee productivity. Employers need to provide facilities that support NEOs' 24/7 mode of operating rather than destroy it. Employee shopping or banking online during 'business hours' is not a corporate price to pay; it is a positive contribution to productivity.

The world is the workplace for NEOs, and NEOs will seek out for themselves the people, technology, facilities, and spirit that support their efforts and contribution. If it happens to come packaged conveniently by a NEO enterprise, the managers of that organisation will be considered potential work associates. When NEOs choose a workplace it is where they go to make relationships, to share ideas and experiences. And they probably only need to go there once a week to achieve this. If they need to go to meetings every day from 9.00 a.m. to 11.00 a.m. for three weeks, that's what they'll do; but they won't be there every day as a matter of course.

This shift in power and focus is a celebration of individual determinism, rather than corporate or employer determinism, because the constructive outcomes are shared.

Such outcomes are also good for the people who pay for their services, whether they are clients or the people formerly known as employers.

For some time, Traditional managers have been grappling with the problem of managing and supporting individuality. Because NEOs are more likely to be found in professional and white-collar positions they are a significant part of any professional workforce (typically more than half). But the challenge is in successfully managing both NEOs and Traditional employees in the one workplace.

Just as NEOs dislike the traditional workplace formula, Traditionals will not be comfortable with the inflexibility and incentives that deliver value and satisfaction to NEOs. The Traditional 50 per cent of the workforce won't want change, will wait for instructions before acting, and will act only within the corporate or role boundaries set for them. The NEO 50 per cent will pace like caged lions if they're placed in this situation, and will either operate outside the established boundaries or create unwanted and unnecessary complexity within the boundaries to keep themselves and their colleagues challenged. NEOs, for example, will react badly to a dress code instruction whereas Traditionals will say, 'Oh good, now I don't have to make a decision.'

The answer lies in differential workplace management—applying the principles of dealing differently with people in different ways in the workplace. This is not a complex approach, but it is demanding.

NEOs turn work into anything they want it to be, and managers need to stop specifying the manner in which they work; stop specifying standard dress codes and cubicle sizes and laptop configurations. One example of the frustrations that NEOs experience in their workplace is the restriction placed on their personal productivity by corporate IT departments that remove user functions from applications such as Microsoft Windows to make them easier to manage from a technical point of view. Having spent many hours personalising these complex tools to suit their individual needs, it is frustrating for a NEO to have all the functions reset to the corporate default settings. The 'one-setting-suits-all' approach, while an exemplar of the efficient traditional workplace, does not work in the NEO workplace.

The message to any manager planning to operate in the NEO economy is, 'Put a NEO in charge so that you can positively restructure the workplace.'

For most large organisations this represents an enormous challenge. But it is a challenge that may well be worth the effort.

We are promised high-resolution video conferencing in our homes and anywhere else we can connect to a mobile or satellite network provider. Therefore, seeing and talking to other people online may soon become a much more satisfying human experience. It is still detached from the experience and energy of human contact, but it is a major improvement over impersonal communication.

Tools for remote group work, supported by video cameras, laptop computers, and the Internet are available now and are becoming commonplace. The websites www.eroom.com and www.hotoffice.com provide tools to any group that can define itself as a team with a common task and information to share.

Even with improved technology, however, you still need spaces that cherish human interaction.

The Future NEO Workplace

The workplace of the future will be part of a larger business village with flexible spaces for working, living, and playing.

An organisation might design a business village or it could buy residential units to lease to NEOs on favourable terms, while just across the lane will be a workplace that bears no resemblance to a traditional office, where NEOs will meet and interact. In this future model, there will be cafés and bars and interesting retail offerings, right where employees live and work. These are not artificially contrived bars evoking memories of the Friday-night drinks in the boardroom. Rather, they are authentic public places where meaningful engagement can take place.

The residences will have large studios attached to them so that NEOs can work at home, either alone or with others in groups. NEOs like to reconfigure the groups they work with and the places and spaces they work in, just as they are likely to reconfigure their residences.

Of course, not everyone will live and work in the same place. Some NEOs will prefer to live in the country or by the sea, and create a virtual business village using the appropriate technology. But, regardless of where they choose to live, NEO enterprises will understand that short-term accommodation in a NEO workplace will create far more powerful productivity than a hotel in a corporate canyon.

An organisation in the future may have as many as one hundred apartments available to employees for short-term, mid-term, or long-term stays. Employees would have the option of moving with their partner and family into the accommodation for a week or a month or a year.

A manager redesigning a large professional-services organisation for NEOs will only have two sorts of spaces: project space and relationship space. The bars and cafés that punctuate the workspaces already provide relationship space.

The project space accommodates the work that people do

together, and there might be a series of individual project rooms for the other work that NEOs are engaged in. Clients, consultants, support staff, and contractors all come together in this project-specific space.

Outside the work-specific project spaces, learning spaces will provide fresh opportunities for people needing other forms of stimulation.

The NEO workplace is no longer a place exclusively for work. The future is not hot-desking an office building, but 'hot-housing' an entire work community by changing the home and the workplace.

6

NEOs at Home

Home is an important form of expression for NEOs and a way of exploring who they are in an evolving world. Compared to Traditionals, NEOs are much more likely to change their houses as life evolves. Changing houses is not, however, just an expression of boredom with the last house; it's a necessary sign that they're evolving. A NEO may remark to herself, 'The textures, colours, and spaces that once suited me no longer reflect who I am. As I evolve and change, I either have to move house, or change the house I'm living in to enable the next stage of life to unfold.'

It is unlikely that a NEO would ever have a house or a house design/layout that lasts more than ten years. Because they're connected with and influence the evolving world, coming home to something that no longer reflects that world and their place in it would create disharmony. So, paradoxically, harmony requires change. NEOs are comfortable with this paradox.

Home provides NEOs with control and individuality. Sometimes, in the complex and evolving world in which they eagerly immerse themselves, they can briefly lose their sense of self. Home, however, is the space that uniquely reflects who they are and realigns their personal compass. Home is intensely personal to NEOs because they have defined it. Home has not defined them; instead it is a handmade, unique space that they have created—either temporarily or permanently. NEOs imbue their house with their values and characteristics. Their home reflects who they are.

Conversely, the house defines Traditionals; it says more about their personality than it says about the house. The house defines who the Traditional is.

By contrast, NEOs typically will either choose a home that is architecturally designed, providing individuality, or they'll look for something historic that brings an evocation of authenticity, a connection with an industrial, agrarian, or maritime heritage—something with a character that reflects their spirit and provides a sense of place.

As NEOs move through life's stages, they use a house or apartment to 'try things on' until their style palate has matured and defined itself. In a sense, this is true of everyone, but NEOs always have a sense of who they are at any particular moment. For example, long before they have the income and the asset base to create something that fully reflects their evolved spirit, NEOs still make choices that reflect their style. Home is somewhere physical to put their individual stamp.

The challenge of searching for a new house is the thrill of finding and creating a place to put a personal stamp. Homewares increasingly enable them to change the personality of a home at will—by changing, for example, the colour and feel of special rooms. This is a root cause of the success of homewares in recent years, and a signpost to their continued success well into the future. Without realising it, NEOs are future-proofing the homewares sector with their evolving appetite for style, and their need to regularly recreate their home environment.

NEOs use their home for resting and healing to find

balance in a complex and changing life. So they will not reward a business that fails to empathise with life's complexity.

NEOs also use their home the way they use clothes—to express what they stand for and to symbolise their sense of style. This is not conspicuous consumption but, rather, the sharing of insights into a personality. A handmade pair of shoes recognised only by another wearer of handmade shoes is a type of secret code. There are secret symbols, sacred symbols, that only NEOs and their fellow NEOs recognise in the arcane language of whispered secrets.

Traditionals will visit a house and see it as a house. NEOs see a house as a window into the personality and values of the owner.

When visitors 'leaf through' a NEO's home, the experience is akin to a secret handshake. When other NEOs study the bookshelf and music collection, they discover much more than mere books and music: they gain a unique glimpse of a personality profile, and learn instantly how to relate.

Such 'filters' are used constantly by NEOs in the myriad judgments and decisions they make on a daily basis. Their home and the homes of their NEO friends are full of arcane codes that are visible and recognisable only to other NEOs.

There is an explosion of interest in aromatherapy, Japanese wishing stones, kitchen gardens, and other handmade ways of not just finding balance, but finding it at home. This embracing of the handmade sense of spiritual balance is another way for NEOs to reconnect with who they are. A NEO's home becomes a form of private chapel, a sacred space into which they admit people who are precious to them.

NEOs no longer invite business people home just for the sake of it, and they certainly don't have huge, anonymous parties. In fact, they are unlikely to stage formal dinner parties any more. They would much rather have people they value staying for the weekend, and marking the occasion with wonderful things to eat and drink—all very relaxed and casual.

Location

Home for a NEO is likely to be in an inner-urban, country, or sea-change location—one that reflects their individual qualities.

The highest concentration of NEOs anywhere in Australia is in the Southbank neighbourhood of Melbourne. In 1991, when redevelopment of the area began (guided by one of the authors of this book), it was a brown-field, post-industrial site with little or no residential development of any kind. But by then NEOs had emerged and had been identified in attitudinal and behavioural research as individuals requiring something completely different from the traditional approach to a commercial development. So the first new village or NEO neighbourhood in Australia was created at Southbank, combining residential, commercial, and cultural elements just for NEOs.

Within a few years of its initial success, unprecedented and unimagined residential development mushroomed around the original development, and the neighbourhood achieved its record NEO concentration in less than a decade.

NEOs, while they are urban dwellers, are also likely to escape to the beach or the bush. When compared to the Australian population as a whole, twice as many NEOs have holiday homes.

When they are home, they like to celebrate the passing of the day with a stiff drink. Almost half proudly declare that they drink more wine than they used to—which, compared to only 29 per cent of the general population, is significant. Red wine is their tipple of preference, with a particular fondness for cabernet sauvignon. The home is their favoured place to enjoy it.

Facilities

Facilities to be found in the home, now and in the future, range from the handmade to the technologically sublime. Technology is moving quickly to place control in the hands of individuals. NEOs are likely to already have in their home interactive television, interactive DVDs, voice-activated computers, wireless broadband, 3G mobile phones, and personal digital assistants (PDA) that have converged with email-enabled mobile phones—all designed to give NEOs more of their cherished control and longed-for freedom.

They will have, or at least will have considered, MP3 music players such as the Apple iPod, and digital cameras connectable directly to printers and laptops from which they instantly email images to friends across the world. NEOs are already questioning why owning a desktop computer is necessary at all, as digital functions merge with other life-related appliances and systems. The spectre of a permanent box on a desk is quickly becoming redundant in the NEO household.

What unifies these techno-aids is that they all put the individual at the centre of his or her own universe.

These products and systems are designed for people who don't wish to accept someone else's view of what music they should be listening to, what television programs they should be watching, or what stories they should be reading. If they only want tracks three, seven, and 15 from the CD, why can't they have only those three? Why can't they have a laptop that delivers music and movies when and how they want them, rather than when a free-to-air channel or movie-distribution company says so? All these technologies are enabling people to control their lives in addition to giving them the freedom to consume when and how they wish.

Because NEOs are smart people they expect smart facilities. So, on the drive home they can call ahead and set the 'climate' at home; and because they don't have a regular schedule, it may be at a different time every day. Technology needs to respond to change and unpredictability in the world of NEOs.

A Traditional also values 'domestic' technology, but concentrates on items such as popcorn machines, bread-makers, rice cookers, and home-brewing beer kits. To our Traditional, they give the impression of being invaluable time-saving appliances, even though they aren't.

They certainly help fill time, and they create a sense of 'getting the job done'; but, in true Traditional style, it is the transaction rather than the experience that is motivating. A NEO, on the other hand, prefers experience over transaction, and chooses to make bread by hand as a therapeutic activity. Or she enjoys the experience of buying a fabulous loaf from her local village baker.

Home for NEOs is a changing place. The challenge is to understand how the home is evolving and what makes it such a wonderful place for them. It may appear counter-intuitive, but change and wonder are everyday experiences for NEOs.

7

The NEO Neighbourhood

We know that NEOs and Traditionals are as different as white truffles and button mushrooms. So it will come as no surprise to discover that NEOs, in wanting to be with others who share their values and attitudes, also yearn for the human scale and individuality offered by the new village or NEO neighbourhood.

When NEOs imagine their ideal place to live, work, and play they will be drawn to the NEO neighbourhood. And if the rest of the world hasn't yet caught up with their innovative thinking, NEOs will figure out a way to make their ideas a reality anyway.

To be successful a NEO neighbourhood must reflect some of the personality traits of NEOs—such as individuality, authenticity, intimacy, edginess, technology, complexity, change, and evolutionary velocity.

In creating a journey for NEOs, it is essential to know how they would like to work, live, and play. They may not always achieve their dream exactly; but those who recognise the NEOs' ambition and take them closer to their perfect place will win their loyalty.

Home and work are fairly simple concepts. As we have noted, the Third Space replaces the community space we all lost when the developers' bulldozers converted the local sports-ground into a shopping mall.

Imagine, therefore, a NEO neighbourhood in an authentic post-industrial city block that combines work, residence, and Third Space. It has emerging technologies available to every residence and workspace: edgy design, outdoor spaces, and a varied mix of commercial and cultural uses constantly evolving as fashions and needs change.

In various forms, the NEO neighbourhood is already emerging and evolving right now around the world in New York, London, Melbourne, and Berlin. But NEO neighbourhoods are still relatively few and far between, and so most NEOs are fulfilling their need for the characteristics of the NEO neighbourhood through a mix of the actual and the virtual. NEOs without physical NEO neighbourhoods are voting with their dollars by visiting the evolving village and street spaces that resemble their dream of a better place, free from shopping malls and theme bars.

While the three elements of work, home, and leisure must all be present to create the true NEO neighbourhood, all three elements do not have to be in a physical village. For example, a NEO may live in an inner-city apartment in Melbourne but work remotely using the rapidly emerging 'web-commuting' technology that makes this possible. The leisure activities that feed the individual NEO's soul may well be enjoyed on the street or online. This virtual convergence of the three elements provides an alternative to the more demanding task of creating an entirely physical NEO neighbourhood.

In its physical shape the NEO neighbourhood gives us insights into the look and feel of the places in which NEOs wish to be. This is the place where a NEO wakes up each morning, starts up her computer, downloads the latest music collection, strolls downstairs to the edgy cafe for coffee and a feisty discussion about Stephen Soderbergh's latest film, and then heads across the laneway to join work colleagues for a strategy workshop in the project-space.

She uses the Internet to read what others are saying about her favourite author's latest novels, browses through reviews, and then decides to make a purchase. She chooses the experience ahead of the transaction. Traditionals, on the other hand, don't recognise any separation between transaction and experience. When they shop at the mall they gain a positive sense of satisfaction. To a Traditional, the very act of shopping is entertaining. This is not so for our NEO and her fellow NEOs. For them, the experience of shopping can be rewarding, but it is far from being enough. They need a strong experience filled with information and challenge and, perhaps, a transaction at the end of it.

So the NEO neighbourhood is much more complex than the local shopping mall. Traditional corporations may not be able to distinguish between experience and transaction space, but NEOs are very clear about the difference.

The entry point into the NEO neighbourhood, either the physical or conceptual one, is therefore through an experience. The NEO neighbourhood has a heart where NEOs look for experiences and rich information. The rare and delicious food on display at David Jones' Bondi Junction Foodhall generates consumption arousal in NEOs. A visitor has a wonderful experience just being in the busy store chatting with the informative staff and discovering new ways to cook and new things to eat. A NEO would find it almost impossible to leave the store without buying something.

The redevelopment by the Sydney Foreshore Authority of a former container wharf on East Darling Harbour promises to provide Australia's best example of a NEO neighbourhood.

The plans for the East Darling Harbour redevelopment include cultural spaces, active and passive parklands, innovative retail outlets, sustainable office environments, and different forms of housing, cafes, restaurants, and bars—all on the waterfront, but fully integrated into the rest of the city. This 22-hectare expansion of Sydney's CBD promises to epitomise the NEO neighbourhood elements of life, work, and play.

Taking a look at a few of the defining factors of a NEO neighbourhood provides insights into the shape of future cities and the opportunities afforded by the new village—wherever it is.

Human Scale in Form and Function

NEOs don't trust monolithic institutions, so a defining characteristic of the NEO neighbourhood is human scale. NEOs reject the traditional authority of the institution and its symbols of power, including the office canyons of the great cities and the world of global brands. We are witnessing a NEO-led move away from the concept of institutional authority in its physical form. We see it daily in the shift in consumer preference away from the ubiquitous shopping mall to the human-scale village or to its ultimate expression, the NEO neighbourhood.

Bulk and height in commercial or even cultural architecture are significant because they represent institutional rather than human values. The Guggenheim Museum in New York City is an oasis nestled in the high-rise canyons of Manhattan. Yet when compared with the Peggy Guggenheim Museum housed in her former residence on Venice's Grand Canal, it is positively monolithic.

Human scale, by definition, allows humans to feel relevant, to grasp and relate to the volume of a space. We are in control of whether or not we will have the sun on our face. Conversely, in large institutional-scale spaces, someone else makes those decisions for us. We have none of the choices we cherish as individuals. Architects and engineers—and their institutional masters—have decided for us what kind of light we'll get, the quality of air we breathe, the temperature of the day, and when we will be given access.

Applied to physical buildings, it is more rewarding for architects and more profitable for businesses to develop human-scale structures that allow natural light and elements to penetrate the spaces in and between buildings. It is more profitable because NEOs will respond well to businesses housed in such spaces; this gives them not only high-margin revenue but also the rarest of prizes in the modern business world—genuine loyalty.

And since the rules that apply in the physical also apply in the virtual, an online place must bring the same approach to its 'architecture' for it to be similarly rewarded. Online sites across the board tend to be more human scale, and that's a contributing factor to NEOs' preference for the Internet. However, NEOs expect a website that not only feels 'hand-made' but also takes them on a personalised and individualised tour of discovery across the landscape of human-scale experiences and opportunities.

Engagement and Relevance

Engagement

Engagement, in its most basic form, refers to human contact and the making of a connection. Without engagement we cannot develop a partnership or a relationship. It seems self-evident that we spend our lives engaging with each other and with what we need, but this is not always entirely so.

Engagement in the urban landscape is rare. The urban paradox is that the closer we get to each other physically, the more distant we become emotionally. In the cities that dot the globe we often don't speak to, or even acknowledge, other people in lifts; we may ignore people we recognise in the street; and we generally only engage with other drivers when we are experiencing a fit of road rage. Modern life disengages us from each other.

On the other hand, in the country village of our dreams we say 'hello' to people we recognise, and even pause to pass on and receive vital pieces of information about what's going on in our small world. We engage with each other and we engage with the products that we wish to buy. In the idealised village the local newspaper is full of small pieces of information including vegetable-planting times, the weather, news of a local car theft, and other local insights. And this feels much more engaging and relevant to us than news of the national political situation or a hundred deaths in a flooded, faraway country.

The formula is simple: human scale + relevance = engagement.

But why is engagement so important in the first place?

International garment manufacturer and retailer Ralph Lauren specialises in creating stores that feel like a country home. The Upper East Side store in Manhattan is a good example of human scale and relevance, packed as it is with country house artefacts designed to transport the customer to a smaller world of quality and elegance that, by buying a Ralph Lauren shirt, the customer feels he or she can partake of a little.

That same Ralph Lauren shirt displayed in the middle of the expansive floor of a Myer department store is just a shirt among hundreds of other shirts; because it doesn't offer the promise of a seductive, albeit perhaps out-of-reach world, it becomes purely a transactional piece of merchandise. While it might be relevant to our immediate needs, it has lost the human scale of the textural, reassuring atmosphere of the Upper East Side store. As a consequence, the shirt in the traditional department store fails to engage us.

The Ralph Lauren store has been created for NEOs; the department store, by its very nature, is for both Traditionals and NEOs. The engaging specialty store has made a distinction between the two social types, and has set about creating a direct and enduring relationship with NEOs. The department stores that fail to recognise the influence of NEOs will either become discount department stores or disappear altogether.

Approached in the right way, even a shirt lost in the crowd of department store merchandise can still be engaging. Imagine Ralph Lauren personally signing a large piece of white card on which is written the story of the Ralph Lauren big shirt. With this simple device, human scale is joined to the pre-existing relevance of the shirt for the customer, and the result is an engaging experience created by a personal connection. This authentic device also converges personality with engagement. Ralph Lauren's own words on a simple piece of card invite engagement with the passing customer, and create a dialogue with a real person about a real story.

But engagement can also be more immediate. When NEOs connect to a contact-centre they should be engaging with people just like them; but, more frequently, they're connecting to a random cross-section of the population, few of whom are likely to be NEOs or understand the qualities of NEOs.

Relevance

Relevance is judged by the degree to which a business can align its offering to the characteristics of the different types of consumer.

For NEOs, an organisation that has a high degree of relevance is one that matches their expectations and aspirations, and is capable of building a relationship. But given that it must evolve, it is not sufficient just to be relevant *now*; it must be relevant over time and evolve with its customers.

In the online world, relevance was initially higher because much of the content was created *by* NEOs *for* NEOs, and we could all discover interesting experiences that weren't available in the physical world. Over time, that relevance has diminished as the Internet has become a more corporate environment.

Many corporations have turned their Internet channel from an authentic, evolving space, in which individual and complex people were open to relationships, into a poor facsimile of the physical world where corporations treat everybody the same. Corporate sites increasingly filter, control, and manage the messages that are on their websites. And NEOs will punish them for the loss of relevant engagement by seeking experiences elsewhere.

Any organisation wishing to conduct transactions in the NEO neighbourhood must subordinate its desire to control. Hard as it is to do so, they must submit to the NEOs' will to determine their own experiences, transactions, and outcomes.

Conflict and contrast

Conflict and contrast stimulate NEOs. They challenge NEOs in the NEO neighbourhood, and NEOs love a challenge. In the everyday world we have become accustomed to static or sanitised environments, so what excites NEOs is contrast and even conflict.

Examples of this can be found in commercial and cultural spaces, residential designs, and workplace layouts. For instance, a developer could use different architects, each using unique approaches, to design a variety of residential zones within a NEO neighbourhood. No effort would be made to tie the separate architects to a theme.

Throughout the development, they could create a positive tension between design approaches and finishes, with raw concrete walls contrasting with super-finished spun steel.

In the retail spaces, experience needs to be at the forefront, so traditional theming of retail or restaurant space would be banished. Rather, a wonderful butcher shop, for example, might be located next to a hip fashion store, next to a laundry, an Asian grocery, an Italian café, and an extreme sports shop.

Commercial spaces would compete with cultural spaces, and each side wins in this new village in which street performers might fly vertically rather than being bound by gravity; fire festivals are staged in winter; and, once a year, tables and chairs, bars, coffee pots, wine barrels, and acrobats tumble out into the streets for a 'Spill Festival'.

It is the tension, the challenge, contrast, change, and evolution that NEOs find attractive and stimulating in an otherwise 'safe and bland' world. This sense of excitement draws them to the NEO neighbourhood.

The Shape of Things to Come

The NEO neighbourhood often evolves organically, fuelled by the NEOs' deep desire for human scale, relevance, and engagement. But for those wishing to develop a NEO neighbourhood from scratch, there are simple lessons to be learned.

Organic evolution

Colin Tudge, in his wonderfully imaginative book *The Engineer in the Garden,* talks ironically of genetic engineering being no more precise than gardening. Similarly, in the NEO neighbourhood the rules of change and evolution are blurred, unpredictable, and imprecise. But one lesson learned from history is that organic evolution, or change over time, is an important factor in the NEO neighbourhood. And while a newly created neighbourhood may not immediately have authenticity, it must reject all artificiality.

Even the purpose-built should draw authenticity from its heritage. That heritage could be industrial, maritime, or rural. The great neighbourhoods that have grown up organically and can be considered NEO neighbourhoods, such as Greenwich Village in New York and Daylesford in Victoria, evolve in an unpredictable and anarchic way. Immediately they become predictable, usually as the result of commercial interests cashing in on the NEOs' spending power, they lose their authenticity, relevance, contrast, and engagement and, as a result, become of little interest to the very consumers the commercial interests came hunting. In these circumstances, the NEO neighbourhood stops being organic, and its diversity is lost. It is the organic growth of the unplanned NEO neighbourhood that creates its rich diversity and contrast.

The NEO neighbourhood also has enigmatic, blurred, physical, and metaphorical boundaries. It eschews the formality of the shopping mall with well-marked entry and exit points, just as it rejects the rules of the civic building with an identifiable shape and position in a streetscape. Rather, it is a neighbourhood that meanders and sprawls, with discoveries to be made around every mysterious and unexpected corner. Australia's best example of this is found in the James Street precinct in Fortitude Valley, Brisbane.

For a NEO neighbourhood to develop organically, the right set of pre-existing NEO conditions must be in place. In New York City, the art galleries that for decades have been the soul of SoHo have moved to the former trucking district of Chelsea. They had moved to SoHo originally because the rents were low, and it was an edgy, authentic neighbourhood with a thriving artist community.

Today, SoHo has more global-brand retail stores than art galleries, and the neighbourhood resembles a linear shopping mall.

Nearby Chelsea, on the other hand, is still genuinely edgy and risky and, as a consequence, rents are lower and the experience is more affordable. The galleries and NEOs have moved into the Chelsea warehouse spaces and lofts that once serviced trucks, drivers, and their mechanics. They are converting these warehouses into new spaces that make a statement about individuality and diversity rather than the more homogenised sleekness of the new SoHo.

The lesson from Chelsea is that a NEO neighbourhood has to be edgy or unconventional, evolving, and diverse. In Melbourne, the inner-city Fitzroy area was, in living memory, a slum notorious for its brothels and petty criminals. Now it is a NEO neighbourhood with a high density of NEO residents (20 per cent greater than the Australian national average).

Every world city has good examples of risky, on-the-edge areas becoming the hip areas of today. But those that go on to become residentially gentrified or overtly commercial lose their edge and, as a consequence, their value. In San Francisco, artists and galleries were forced out of the downtown Bay Area when, during the original tech boom, property values escalated and the artists and gallery owners could no longer afford the rents. High-rise blocks will ultimately replace desirable heritage buildings, and the property cycle will turn. How many great cities have expensive high-rise towers that have forced out the residents and left the city with no heart and no activity outside office hours, only to see those high-values evaporate as quickly as the residents leave?

A sense of *escape* is another pre-condition for the organic emergence of a NEO neighbourhood. It can be to an edgy inner-city neighbourhood, a country town, or a seaside village where a new style of work, housing, and leisure converge in a new way.

If an urban district fails to offer a sense of escape, the result will be an inevitable shift of NEOs to the bush or the beach.

How does such a sea-change NEO neighbourhood emerge?

A NEO sea change/tree change

Imagine this scenario: over a period of a year or two, six NEO couples move to the beach or the bush. They are individualists looking for the authentic and the unconventional, and have sought it by moving away from the city. But proximity to work and culture is important to them.

One-and-a-half hour's travel to the city is about the limit. After all, NEOs lead busy lives and don't want to cut themselves off from the culture of the city. In New York and London, two hours on the excellent rail systems is acceptable. This is, after all, slow time, and NEOs will utilise technology to accelerate it.

However, after our six couples have been commuting for a year or two, they become less interested in the cultural life of the city and more localised in their views and interests.

One or two of them decide to create an opportunity close to where they live by starting a business: a fabulous coffee shop and bookshop. So begins the NEOs' sea-change lifestyle and a NEO neighbourhood.

Authenticity is provided by the history of the area, either rural or maritime, and by the natural heterogeneity and contrast that these people find in their village — the butcher next to the fashion store, next to a small printing workshop, next to the dry-cleaner, and now the fabulous coffee shop next to the great bookshop.

Soon there's a hobby shop and an award-winning deli selling locally produced organic smallgoods and breads, and the new neighbours can walk down the village street and sense the heritage of the place.

By the sea, they observe with pleasure the working fisherman; in the country, they can join a discussion in the high street about beef prices, the weather, or the local heritage gallery's latest exhibition.

The contrast between the urban blandness of traditional cities and the stimulation and authenticity of the newly emerging NEO neighbourhood is marked, and often remarked upon.

The first NEO to open a store sets a precedent. Other NEOs immediately see the opportunity for engagement, while local businesses see that it is possible to succeed by creating a rich experience in the right atmosphere. The first of the new species of business passes on the acquired benefits to others.

If a level of pent-up demand exists in the area for services and experiences that NEOs value, the rate of growth will be rapid enough to get through the sluggish bottom of the growth curve, and the neighbourhood will take off.

A Mature NEO Neighbourhood

Late-stage organic NEO neighbourhoods are most clearly characterised by a clear strategic intent. For example, Napa, north of San Francisco, is a pleasant town in a valley that is almost exclusively devoted to growing grapes and making wine. Everywhere you look you see vineyards. Every sign you see and every business you encounter relates to wine. The entire community is dedicated to the business of wine.

In Napa, a Silicon Valley billionaire bought the old railway—lines, rolling stock, and all. He upgraded it to run a wine tour, where visitors can meet the wine-makers, have lunch, and experience the Napa Valley first-hand. It does not feel like a tourist trap, but instead is an engaging way of exploring and discovering the world of wine-making.

Like the Napa Valley, any area that becomes a NEO neighbourhood must also have something to be 'famous for'. And what it is famous for has nothing to do with promotion or marketing, but rather refers to the soul of the place, a reason to love it—something that makes it deeply authentic and memorable.

Part of the allure and authenticity of a place that is 'famous' for something is often generated by its activity as a working place. Napa is famous for wine, and everywhere there are working examples of its pride and its promise. But it is too large to be a NEO neighbourhood and too small to have NEO neighbourhoods in different parts of town.

Greenwich Village in Manhattan is a more complete example of a late-stage NEO neighbourhood that brings together residential spaces, work, and leisure. Street markets showcase local crafts and food products as local performers delight passers-by. Clear to NEOs are not only the values Greenwich Village symbolises, but also the fact that other NEOs live, work, and play there.

An Australian example can be found in Brisbane's Fortitude Valley. The James Street precinct was created on a former semi-industrial site between the seemingly incurable seediness of Fortitude Valley and the rapidly gentrifying New Farm. Ranging over several blocks, the neighbourhood offers NEOs treasures for the home—from hand-made delicacies for the kitchen to global brands that include Bang & Olufsen, Bose, and Apple, and Australian brands such as Made in Japan, Wheel & Barrow, Space, and Rogerseller. There are places to eat, movies to see, fabulous bars with exceptional wine lists, and a fresh-food market. The residential apartments cement its status as arguably the most interesting NEO neighbourhood in Australia.

The NEO neighbourhood is a manifestation of the principle of diverse solutions for diverse people. It celebrates authenticity and diversity both within its own blurred boundaries and with the broader community in which it exists. A NEO neighbourhood such as James Street is a vital clue to understanding NEOs. It graphically demonstrates how they react, what they like or dislike, and what excites them.

The NEO neighbourhood is the starting place for understanding NEOs, and is the grand opportunity for Australians to create a physical agent of change.

Part Two

NEOs Embracing Life

The New Agenda

On a wintry Wednesday morning, Sarah Fielding walks past the finger wharf in highly urbanised Woolloomooloo in Sydney. A business analyst for one of the recently privatised energy companies, Sarah is accustomed to change. Her life altered when globalisation transformed the energy sector from a sleepy giant into separate, smart, hard-won, and hard-run enterprises. It was this shift in business behaviour that attracted her to an industry that her parents thought dull.

Overnight, the institutions that once set the rules were transforming into enterprises that now asked their customers what the rules should be. Sarah saw the opportunity to make a difference and to create a place for herself. She grabbed it with both hands.

Now the day ahead for Sarah is, like her life, full of the promise of change. And the way she spends her day symbolises the challenge that business faces in this changing world.

Sarah Fielding is part of the new economic order. She's not really aware of it, but she is different from some of her friends and many of her workmates. She is passionately individualistic and quick to embrace personal challenges—living as she does in Woolloomooloo, a breathing contradiction of wealth and poverty, just a stone's throw from Kings Cross, most famous for its drug culture, prostitution, and sex shows, Sarah likes the edginess of her neighbourhood.

She also likes doing things her own way.

Swinging aboard a bus for the short ride to Martin Place, Sarah glances around her, wondering what each of her fellow passengers does for a living. It is a kind of game she plays whenever she gets the chance. Then, deciding to update her tasks for the day, she flips open her iPod, which also contains her calendar, a thousand songs, and more than two hundred contacts. As she opens it, her phone vibrates. (She dislikes intrusive ringing phones in public places.)

It's her travel agent with news of a brand-new adventure-destination in Africa. During the conversation, Sarah gazes at the others on the bus. Sitting next to her is a young woman about her own age — an accountant, Sarah decides, probably an auditor. Georgie Gardner returns Sarah's gaze and studies a face animated by conversations about a kind of holiday that Georgie only enjoys in her daydreams.

Just as Sarah is a NEO, Georgie is a Traditional, characterised by both her abhorrence of change and her personal comfort with life's certainties. Although she is the same age, doesn't earn significantly less than Sarah, and has a professional job, Georgie wants entirely different things out of life. So while Sarah spends five times as much money on clothes, eats out four times more and travels interstate on holidays four times more frequently, Georgie is happy with her lot, acknowledging that her life revolves around less glamorous but, to her, more serious interests.

Sarah's career has always been hard to separate from her personal life. Whatever she does, she takes control and plans every step along the way. Georgie, on the other hand, leaves everything pretty much to chance.

Georgie's career path is really a matter of luck — she calls it being in the right place at the right time. Recently, she has been feeling decidedly unwell, but has done nothing about it. 'Sometimes it's better not to know. Things have a way of sorting themselves out,' she has remarked in an unguarded moment to a colleague at work.

Sarah and Georgie, sitting on the same bus, could not be more different.

Finishing her phone call, Sarah returns to the task menu on her iPod, finishes planning her day, and steps from the bus onto the street, without really understanding that she and millions like her are setting a new agenda.

-8-

Travel: NEOs taking the path less travelled

'We have not finished our journey until we have reached the
beginning again and seen it for the first time.'
T.S. Eliot

There's no consumption choice more discretionary than
leisure travel. Purchases of clothing, food, housing, and transport all have elements of discretionary choice, but they are
much more likely to belong in the basic-needs basket of consumption. The fact is that no one *needs* to travel in order to
enjoy their leisure time.

As it happens, those who do spend the most on travel also
spend the most on other discretionary categories such as
wine, restaurant meals, jewellery, personal and household
services, entertainment, books, music, and homewares. NEOs
dominate all discretionary spending, including travel.

As we have already seen, a high level of discretionary
spending is fuelled by, but is not an automatic consequence
of, high levels of income or wealth. Wealthy consumers cannot
automatically be assumed to be frequent leisure travellers;
and while NEOs are more highly represented in high-income
brackets, not all NEOs who travel frequently are wealthy.

So when we look at the choices NEOs and Traditionals make for their holiday plans and purchases, it's no surprise that they are as different as Swedish and Swahili.

For NEOs, leisure travel is a Third Space experience: a tangible way of connecting with desire, and expressing celebration and discovery. It fuels the spirit and creates new relationships and personal insights. It can be high-tech and high-touch, or low-tech and tactile. It can be a short break or a sabbatical. It can be solitary or intensely peopled. But the one thing it can't be is controlled by a corporation. NEOs are rewriting the rules on leisure and travel just as they are rewriting the rules for home and work. The consumption power of the new economic order is based on individually controlled, personally relevant choices.

For NEOs, the path less travelled is the most seductive because it provides a natural contrast to the realms of work, where the corporation is still king. To explore the outer boundaries of the Third Space—the place that is not work and not home—is immensely satisfying to NEOs. It creates a sense of a larger personal space, and provides the stimulation of new ideas and new perspectives that refresh and recharge the day-to-day.

Of all Australians who travel by air domestically every couple of months, 75 per cent are NEOs and only 10 per cent are Traditionals. NEOs are more than four times more likely to fly on business, but also more than 50 per cent more likely to fly on holidays. Not only are they frequent travellers; they spend more each time they travel than anyone else in the economy. They are more than twice as likely as Traditionals to spend between $5,000 and $7,500 on a holiday of three or more nights, and three times more likely to spend in excess of $10,000 when they do.

Australians say the kind of holiday they most enjoy is

either 'rest and relaxation' or is outdoors-focused. N
more than just the basics from their holidays. That
dominate the more purposeful and specialist holiday ᴄᴀᴛᴇ₋ᵤ
ries such as food, wine, and health tourism.

Traditionals tend to use their leisure time as a way of filling
in mandatory weeks of spare time away from the job that
defines them. Not so for NEOs. It is a project to be invested
in, researched, planned, and experienced in a way that creates
new heights of pleasure and new boundaries of personal
knowledge and satisfaction. A holiday is an experience driven
by deep desire.

Take Sarah Fielding: she has fallen in love with Africa. She
hasn't been there yet, but she has already immersed herself in
its magic. She invested emotional and intellectual effort in
dreaming about and researching her next holiday, beginning
her relationship with this new continent long before she
physically arrives there.

It all started with a whispered secret—in conversation
with a group of friends over dinner. A university friend had
just returned from a stint with Medecins Sans Frontières in
Sudan, and was painting a picture of the stark contrasts
between despair and privilege, between desert and jungle,
and between her sense of herself as an individual and the
overwhelming fact of her insignificance among the teeming
masses of humanity. When the conversation turned to the
subject of how to live, where to stay and where to eat, she
described a beautiful guest house outside one of the capital
cities that she'd fallen for and returned to whenever she'd
had a break from her medical duties. It gave her, she remarked
warmly, a sense of the beauty and the authentic rhythm of
day-to-day life that Africa could offer. Sarah could feel the
hairs standing on the back of her neck. She was hooked:
hooked on the idea of contrasts, of pleasure and pain, of the

sacred and profane. She needed to discover how she would deal with these contrasts. She needed to experience the magic of Africa for herself.

Georgie Gardner is also fascinated with Africa. She and her family treated themselves to tickets to the Lion King stage show when it came to Sydney. They loved the music, and played the soundtrack endlessly for a couple of weeks. They've even been to the Western Plains Zoo in Dubbo to see the African animals in their open surroundings, and they've talked about going on a safari tour one day because it would be one of those once-in-a-lifetime things to do. But there are concerns about language and security and sanitation. The risks are too great, and they don't know anyone who lives there who might provide a familiar face and protection against being ripped off. The tried-and-true is what attracts Georgie; after all, you don't want to waste your hard-earned holiday money on experimentation. The unsettling conundrum for Georgie in choosing a holiday is that you can never be sure that you're getting value for your money until it's over.

Sarah, on the other hand, reflects a few key NEO characteristics when she considers travelling.

Individuality is power

NEO travellers insist on individuality. They don't easily trust large institutions that treat them as part of a 'target group' or market segment. Wherever there is a choice between doing something that enriches them as individuals and something that suits a corporation or institution, NEO travellers will choose the former.

Remember, NEOs have a high *locus of control* so they see themselves as the architects of their own life experiences. They want an itinerary that lets them plan, puts them in control, and incorporates their individual interests and preferences. While they will happily divulge personal details to someone they trust, NEOs are unhappy about filling out standard forms or giving more than basic personal details to a booking agent or receptionist. They are reluctant to follow standard processes; instead, they will ask, 'Why can't I do it like this? My way!'

NEOs generally question the information provided in brochures and insist on speaking to someone in charge (or with personal experience) rather than a front-line employee who is giving them the standard pitch on the best holiday package. They will remove brand names and labels from 'free' travel bags or other travel industry giveaways. They prefer to use a Lonely Planet guide or *Australian Gourmet Traveller* tips to plan an independent trip rather than take a pre-paid, all-inclusive tour with a corporate travel company.

Personalisation outranks customisation

Customisation occurs when a business takes a set of pre-existing products and services and *bundles* them for specific groups or segments—for example, to baby boomers, families, opera enthusiasts, or young people interested in extreme sports. Conversely, personalisation occurs when a business responds in a unique or idiosyncratic way to *individual* requirements and expectations—offering a different response to each individual customer each time they deal with the company.

NEOs are motivated by personalisation, and will seek it out as a priority in their travel choices. They are the restaurant customers who pay more for options that offer an idiosyncratic set of choices; choosing, for example, a menu recommended by the chef but happily paying extra to get the dessert they want from the a la carte menu. They frequent hotels that notice, record, and remember individual guest preferences such as pillow type or furniture placement. They will only consider a packaged tour when it explicitly and demonstrably values them as individuals.

While NEOs dislike and distrust loyalty schemes, they are Australia's most ardent frequent-flyer members. Almost half of all NEOs are members of a frequent-flyer plan compared to only 11 per cent of Traditionals. And NEOs make up 62 per cent of the Qantas frequent-flyer program in Australia.

The most frequently missed opportunity in frequent-flyer schemes is the ability to recognise the propensity to *spend* as distinct from the propensity to *fly*. Because so many frequent-flyer points are earned through business travel, which is generally bought through volume deals and arrangements by corporate purchasing officers, airlines cannot distinguish between truly valuable individuals and valuable corporations.

Sarah Fielding and Georgie Gardner have both recently become platinum-level frequent flyers with Qantas. They both fly regularly for their jobs — Sarah attends meetings about pricing changes with energy regulators, and Georgie travels to client offices and sites around the country in her role as an auditor. They were both delighted to finally get recognised by Qantas as valuable customers, and both have had occasion to be glad that platinum status gives them a better chance of rescheduling flights when there are delays or cancellations. To Qantas, they look identical because they travel so much; but that's where the similarity ends between these two frequent flyers.

Georgie is delighted with the *free* benefits of her platinum status. It provides her with membership of the Qantas Club and access to its lounges, where she can take full advantage of the free food. She now organises more meetings with her colleagues in the business lounges because it's cheaper and easier than meeting for a coffee in the city.

Sarah is also happy with her benefits, but wishes she could order her preferred breakfast pre-flight via the Internet; check her luggage in at one end and have it delivered to her hotel at the other; automatically book a reliable executive taxi for her onward trip when she books her flights; and even wishes she could pick up a healthy, fresh, and interesting dinner at the end of the flight to take home and eat with her boyfriend, rather than eating a meal on the plane when she could use the in-flight time to catch up on work. She can't imagine why having an executive chef such as Neil Perry from Sydney's famed Rockpool restaurant is an advantage on Qantas if she's only being offered a choice of the same two salmon or chicken meals on every flight she's taken in the last 12 months.

The most important difference is that Sarah would be happy to pay a premium to Qantas for her preferred services while Georgie feels it's a privilege just to get the basic benefits. Qantas has got it right for Traditionals, but could be generating significantly higher margins and revenues from Australia's four million NEOs—and making them happier flyers in the process. The challenge for Qantas is to discover which frequent flyer is which.

Relationship outranks transaction

Although NEO travellers spend more, and more frequently, that doesn't make the transaction central to them. Their actual experience is far more important than the transaction, and the relationships developed during the experience extend that pleasure, pushing the mere transaction further into the background.

Naturally, the financial or business transaction is vital for commercial success, but many businesses believe it is the beginning and the end; they behave in a price-based, feature-driven transactional way; but, while this is appropriate for Traditional tourists, it is a serious turn-off to NEO travellers.

A satisfactory (and profitable) transaction with a NEO traveller will follow automatically from a rich and successful purchasing experience. For Traditionals, however, the transaction *is* the experience.

To highlight the difference, Georgie will call three travel agents and say that he has $2,000 to spend on a holiday on the Gold Coast, adding that he wants the best bang for the buck—the most holiday for his money. He will then compare the offers and choose the one that has the most features per dollar. He wants the best deal, and the best deal is represented by the price—a proxy for a bundle of features.

Conversely, Sarah will have decided in advance what kind of holiday she wants by researching on the Internet and talking to friends. She may have been inspired by a beautiful image in a travel magazine, an anecdote, or a tip from another NEO. If she decides to call her favoured travel agent to make the task easier or more efficient, she'll simply say, 'I've fallen in love with Mollies' luxury boutique hotel in Auckland. It was named best new small hotel in the world by Harper's *Hideaway Report* for 2005, and this is what I understand the options are. Can you confirm with them that I can do these five things and, while you're at it, get me the best price?'

Everyone wants the best deal. Everyone wants the best price. The difference between these two travel examples has to do with where the price or the deal sits in the conversation. Traditionals always start with price; for NEOs, price is just the cost of satisfying deep desire, of falling in love.

As the travel industry has transformed itself through global supply arrangements and the aggregation of agents and packages, its product and brand communications have focused consumers on price-based and feature-based comparisons. As a result, they have succeeded in encouraging more Traditionals to book through them. Traditionals are now two times more likely to book their travel with a travel agent than they are to use the Internet.

But in their pursuit of volume and efficiency, travel agents have broken the nexus between the travel agent as a personal travel facilitator and the NEO as a frequent and profitable travel customer. The intensely personal interactions with an individual travel agent that used to characterise the holiday-purchase process have been replaced by NEO travellers acting as the coordinator of a series of transactional interactions on the Internet or with disparate agents and providers across the globe. It's no surprise, then, that travel agents are now ranked third behind the Internet and friends and family as influencing NEOs' travel choices.

NEO travellers, because of their wide range of spending experiences, know what distinguishes a good transaction from a bad one. They are deeply suspicious of a 'free gift' or an up-front discount, believing it is the sign of a transactional operator rather than a new friend with whom they can start a relationship.

NEOs want to know the people and the stories behind the travel experience; they want to feel involved in a personal way with the people who are handling their money. They often request a specific staff member when they call or visit or, in the case of first contact, are skilled at filtering different staff until they get the 'right one'. And when they have found someone who makes a connection, who can listen and understand personal and idiosyncratic holiday intentions, who can help to create an itinerary that is personally relevant, the NEO treasures the relationship and rewards it with loyalty. By this stage of the NEO–agent process, the price of the options is low on the purchase criteria. NEOs, once they have been attracted to someone who understands, will pay a premium for this rare and satisfying experience. And then they bring their friends to make personal introductions for them. In this way, relationships create relationships. And NEO relationships are more profitable than others.

Information is oxygen

NEO travellers are never likely to say that they suffer from information 'overload'. They thrive on information. Without information they would be starved of new ideas and perspectives that stimulate and vitalise them, and which they constantly use to redefine who they are. For NEO travellers, information is a shortcut to a rich and satisfying experience.

NEO travellers are the explorers of both the physical world *and* the online world. They are willing to try new food, new cultures, new experiences, and new technology; but, first and foremost, they need good information. And, because information provides a pathway through complexity, it also reduces the risk of a bad experience and is therefore a critical link in the NEO chain of experience.

The Internet is the travel-information source of choice for NEOs. They are more than four times more likely to use the Internet for researching and planning a holiday than Traditionals. For NEOs, the Internet is the archetypal advisor: full of options and complexity; full of tangential links that provide surprises and rare chances to connect with someone or somewhere entirely new and unpredictable; yet reassuringly full of facts, figures, and contact details that aid decision-making.

NEOs are 80 per cent more likely than Traditionals to use a guidebook to influence their choice of holiday. When planning a trip they will buy a Lonely Planet, a Dorlan Kindersley, *and* a Rough Guide to compare information on a particular destination. They will already have searched the website they're interested in, as well as several others, to get information before they call to ask the first question. When they call, therefore, they will expect to speak to 'an expert' rather than a typical front-line employee who may not have the knowledge to give detailed, personalised information. NEOs are well informed, and they expect this to be acknowledged in their relationships with travel providers. One of a NEO's most obvious 'buying' signals is the quiver of excitement that follows the discovery of a travel provider who not only provides rich information but also offers whispered secrets.

Authenticity is emblematic

In an increasingly transactional world, NEO travellers are reacting by seeking authentic experiences. It is becoming harder for everyone to find real and trusted experiences among the glib offerings developed and promoted by travel corporations. Authenticity is achieved when the people who *know* connect with people who *care* about that knowledge.

Farm holidays, wilderness experiences, and genuine eco-tourism align with NEOs' desire for authenticity in a natural setting. They love the fact that the owners would still be running, for example, an organic farm—even if there were no travellers. This is a good rule of thumb for authenticity used by NEO travellers: the sense, the belief, the expectation that 'they would still be doing what they're doing even if no one came'.

Consider also this test of authenticity: an Irish theme pub in Australia is inauthentic, but a local pub run by an Irishman who is passionate about Guinness served with fried cabbage and bacon is authentic. The difference is found in the people, and their intent and their integrity. These people, these 'authentic' experts, knowledgeable and passionate about their chosen field, are a rich source of experience, relationships, and new knowledge for NEO travellers.

Mollies, the luxury boutique hotel in Auckland, is a shining example of the way that authenticity creates sustainable and profitable connections with NEOs. Mollies wasn't created by travel industry experts who used business analysts to crunch the numbers on the Auckland tourist market and then identify a need for a small luxury hotel. It was created by two smart, urbane world-travellers who decided to come home to New Zealand after decades of living in the most cosmopolitan cities in the world—two talented individuals who wanted to bring their world with them to Auckland and share it with the world of like-minded people. Frances Wilson is internationally celebrated as a voice coach for opera singers, and Stephen Fitzgerald has a life's history of stunning building transformations. Together they have created a unique residence that connects the drama of opera and the drama of place. But it's not just the residence that creates the sense of authenticity; it's that the residence and the experience of staying there stands for something more than just profit. It stands for a way of life—a set of values that encompass beauty, perfection, ambition, challenge, and refinement.

The grand pianos scattered through the suites and public rooms are not token gestures nor are they passive symbols of grand living—they're there to be used at any time of the day to illustrate a musical point in an impromptu conversation between music lovers, or to accompany an intimate opera recital. Visitors don't even need to like opera to get caught up in the excitement and the challenges of the lifestyle of world-class performers who drop in. They don't need to like opera to explore the rich assortment of books, manuscripts, and CDs that reveal the history and the interests of the owners.

They don't need to be opera lovers to appreciate the invitation to share a pre-dinner drink with the man who's described as 'the next Pavarotti'. They don't need to be opera lovers to appreciate the attentions of Tristan, the friendly Burmese who adds elegance and his own personal welcome to the warmth and professionalism of the staff. They don't need to be opera lovers to feel deeply satisfied by the authenticity of the experience that Mollies delivers.

The edge is the place to be

NEO travellers fill their lives with change and evolution, thriving on new and challenging experiences. They seek out the new and different, even if it feels uncomfortable. They are often creators of new experiences and businesses themselves—building success with like-minded friends and colleagues. The time and personal space that is created by going on holiday is a catalyst for discovering something new and different.

Sarah's neighbourhood is an example of an edgy destination. The hotel at the Woolloomooloo finger wharf that started its life as the only W Hotel in Australia sat across the road from a pub with a traditional front bar that expected fist fights on Friday nights. The W Hotel's reception desk was hard to find, and the lighting gave everyone the experience of suddenly being visually impaired. To one side of the wharf, wealth spilled out into the marina full of million-dollar yachts; on the other side was low-cost public housing. This edginess attracted NEOs in their droves to the restaurants, bars, apartments, and the hotel on the wharf. The hotel is no longer a W, and is now known as Blue Woolloomooloo Bay.

Georgie and her Traditional friends would never even know all this existed; and if they did, would never consider visiting.

When they're travelling, NEOs build 'space' into their itinerary because they anticipate discovering something that will absorb and intrigue them—without knowing what it is when they set off. And the experience of the modern world is that the un-signed places are the most likely to be new and different. NEOs reject the well-known and sign-posted in preference for the evolving and emerging—'hip strips' rather than shopping malls, laneways rather than highways, unconventional and alternative rather than the standardised, globalised, and packaged.

Technology accelerates slow time

NEO travellers are heavy users of modern information and communications technology. While they're not necessarily early adopters in the sense of valuing a gadget for its own sake, they will buy anything new that will help them stay in control and manage their time to suit their own style and preferences. NEO travellers are 24/7 people, and believe that technology such as phone and Internet banking exists to enable them to shift time to their advantage. In accelerating slow time (such as the time spent waiting in an airport) with useful services such as banking from Internet-connected mobile phones, NEO travellers also jettison tasks that are mundane and time-consuming. This leaves them more personal time to fill with interesting and challenging experiences and people.

They research and book travel and entertainment online; they pay bills and order guide books online. When planning or booking travel, they send emails late at night in order to avoid sitting in a phone queue waiting for service.

They automate information delivery, using RSS feeds and downloading podcasts, accelerating their knowledge and making more slow time for reflection and research. They have daily news and stock market updates delivered online instead of watching the evening news, but still buy and read the papers on a Saturday. The growing use of radio-frequency identity tags, which make it possible to deliver to their mobile phone relevant and timely information about the latest restaurant reviews and menu options as they walk down a crowded 'eat street' in London, is a logical and welcome extension of travel services to a NEO.

Complexity and paradox are seductive

NEO travellers are comfortable with complexity and paradox, partly because they have the capacity to deal with it and partly because it excites them to be able to 'surf' complexity—never really knowing whether they will ride the wave or be dumped. When they log on to the Internet, they are in their element. After all, the World Wide Web is a complex place filled with paradox.

When they travel, they expect and relish complexity. They reject simplified, streamlined travel packages in favour of challenging personalised itineraries. They always ask 'what if' questions to explore all the possibilities of a given set of offerings or circumstances; and they expect to be provided with more options, not fewer. NEOs will happily relate an apparently chaotic or unexpected mishap in their travels with good humour, because it is remembered as a rich experience rather than a travel disaster. They allow for 'unplanned' time in their itineraries in anticipation of complexity and chaos.

Yet NEOs cannot be pigeon-holed as risk-seeking adventure-lovers who always want the most extreme challenge when they take a holiday. They are equally attracted to the comfort of a global hotel chain—because it provides a reliable base from which to explore and experience other things. NEOs are more than five times more likely than Traditionals to stay in a five-star hotel on holidays. They are seven times more likely than anyone else in the general population to stay at one of the unique hotels in the Small Luxury Hotels of the World (SLH) group, and nine times more likely to stay at a hotel in the Starwood chain (which includes the Westin, Sheraton, and W Hotel brands). Both of these global accommodation groups have built a distinct feature into their offer—clear and sustained differences in every aspect of the experience that each property (in the SLH case) or brand (in the Starwood case) provides its guests.

The most NEO of the Starwood brands, the W Hotels, are designed specifically around the unique features of the property and neighbourhood that they are built in, reflecting and

---

W

Dear Ms. Byth,

Welcome to W Sydney.

Life is all about choices and we are delighted you have chosen to stay with us.

We consider you to be a Very Important Person so we would like to give you a little something during your stay. Naturally we would hate to give you something you didn't like or want, so we would like to invite you to make another choice, for your personal room amenity.

- The W effervescent, aromatherapy bath bomb.
- "Steal something from the Munchie Box".
- Fresh Fruit.
- "Gimme a drink".

Please select from the list above, call "Whatever, Whenever" with your choice and we will take care of the rest.

Have a great stay.

Russell Durnell
Director of Sales & Marketing

amplifying the individual characteristics to cr/
message that individuals are celebrated. If
assistance or information in a W Hotel, they sim₊ .
'whatever, whenever' button on the cordless phone.
Westin Hotels have a 'service express' button on their room
phones and a list of amenities for frequent stayers to choose.
At a W Hotel, however, the amenity is offered as a set of
options with an accompanying message that reinforces the
philosophy that life should be about individual options and
choices, and that the global corporation behind the W Hotel
is able to acknowledge the individual through their processes
and services. This is the paradox that attracts and motivates
NEOs.

Change sets the pace

NEO travellers are not only comfortable with change — they
create it. But for NEOs change must be an evolution, evidence of moving forward and developing.

Change is a fast track to the future rather than a source of
unease about the present. NEOs are confident, and feel free
to carve out their own future and create their own destiny.
They will leave itinerary changes to the last possible date to
ensure they have incorporated the options that are the newest
and freshest.

Travel is the ultimate expression of creating this
destiny — each experience is a measure of moving forward
and discovering something new, as well as a benchmark or a
backdrop for sensing and reflecting on how they have changed
as individuals. NEOs are the most likely to tell their travel
providers, 'Yes I've already tried that. What's new?' It's not
that they want to accumulate 'stamps in their passport' in lieu
of exploring a favourite location in more depth — they want
both. Organic change in a well-loved destination is just as

attractive as a new destination that demonstrates sustainable change.

The paradox that comes with being a NEO is also present in the travel sector. The more NEOs travel, the more they open up new frontiers and experiences for others to follow—and the harder it is to find the authentic new experiences and places in future.

In Australia, the most popular NEO short-stay destinations (for a holiday of one or two nights only) are:

- Sydney
- Hunter Valley
- Victorian Snowfields
- Spa Country (Victoria)
- Noosa

The most popular long-stay destinations (for a holiday of three or more nights) are:

- Mt Hotham
- Falls Creek
- Freycinet National Park
- Margaret River
- Barossa Valley
- Broome
- Cradle Mountain
- Whitsunday Islands
- Uluru
- Port Douglas

Each of these destinations has a well-developed infrastructure for premium travellers, so it is no surprise that NEO travellers favour them. Yet the critical challenge in remaining a sustainable destination for NEOs is always about change. The growth and maturity of an offering has not always been associated with NEO success.

Once an Australian destination is developed well enough to be 'packaged' with standardised offerings on the global market, it becomes more attractive to large volumes of price-sensitive, risk-averse, first-time Traditionals. The brand dominates, and must remain consistent over time; but that consistency must not be allowed to degenerate into sanitisation and sameness. So while Brand Noosa must reliably deliver a relaxed pace with easy access to a clean beach on the edge of a pristine national park, along with a diversity of award-winning restaurants and cafes, there exists an inelastic limit on how many more restaurants and hotel rooms can be built at Noosa before it puts at risk the very elements that attract high-value NEO travellers.

Brand Australia also plays a dominant part in this equation: people choose Australia by comparing its features to, say, Brand USA. And as economic development gathers speed in countries such as China and India and, coincidentally, as economic uncertainty and militarism accelerate in traditional tourism destinations, such as the US and the UK, millions of potential new visitors will turn to Australia—both for its iconic destinations or its relative safety. The economic reality, however, is that we can't send more buses to Freycinet or Uluru, any more than we can accept more development at Uluru.

Travel operators in a volume business will attract Traditionals, and they need to keep expanding the infrastructure that feeds that volume. Smart operators in the high-value NEO market will also evolve and change, but they will simply focus on the quality of the experience rather than the quantity of the bodies through the door. Lodges in New Zealand charge—and receive—nightly rates that would make most Traditionals rush to their bank manager for a loan while simultaneously downing a Valium.

The travel world needs to satisfy the needs of both NEOs and Traditionals. The smart operators, however, are not in business for both.

9

Media and Communications: NEOs connecting with their world

If relishing change is a defining characteristic of the new economic order, media and communications are the nourishment that supports it. NEOs read more books, more specialist magazines, and more national newspapers than anyone else in society. In fact, they dominate the readership of Australia's national newspapers and daily broadsheets. They are also heavy Internet users and magazine readers, but light listeners to commercial radio, and medium viewers of commercial television. Keeping informed is the daily task of NEOs, staying at the crest of the information wave and not being dumped into the wash of trivia, misinformation, and noise that characterises today's mass media and communications sector. The NEO catchcry is, 'Stop shouting; we aren't listening!'

The most significant source of connection to the wider world for NEOs is the Internet. It is their preferred space because it allows them to be who they want to be, to express themselves; to search, discover, and contribute to things that motivate them in their own time and their own way. The Internet is not yet controlled by the corporation, and that makes it one of the rare enablers of individual interests and outcomes. NEOs are heavy Internet users—they make up the majority of all people who use the Internet more than eight times a week. (Traditionals represent only 10 per cent of this group.) The bulk of NEOs have an Internet connection at both home and at work, and more than half of them have broadband or cable connections at home.

Sourcing

NEOs will always assume that they don't have enough information to make a decision; that there is always someone, somewhere in the world, who knows something that they don't, or has access to a fact or insight that is not readily available to the wider population. So the issue is not how much information they can access, but its quality. Reliable sources are vital, but a NEO view is not the same as a Traditional view of a reliable source of information.

Traditionals typically assume that the information they can access is sufficient to make a decision. Because their bias for decision-making is a functional one, they focus on a comparative evaluation of what's available. They have confidence that what is available in the Australian marketplace is of sufficient depth and diversity; that a good deal can be found for almost every item or service that they need.

Traditionals can be genuinely and completely shocked to learn, after the event, that there was much more information that they could have taken into account, and that a whole new deal was waiting to be done. A reliable source of information for a Traditional is the daily newspaper because it is an authoritative source of information, because it belongs to a global industry, because it is run by a large corporation (and therefore its success must rely on providing the best information in the market), and because it has the resources to cover all the news and editorial categories that the average reader expects.

Georgie reads the daily newspaper every morning on the

way to work. It fills in the time on the bus trip and gets the task of keeping-up-to-date out of the way. She has always read the same paper, likes the tabloid format and style of the information, and feels comfortable that the paper reflects what she and the rest of the population are concerned about and interested in. If she gets home early enough, she'll make the effort to watch the nightly commercial current affairs programmes, too, because they give her the inside stories on many of the issues that are covered in the newspaper.

A reliable source of information for NEOs, on the other hand, starts with an evaluation of what that news source 'stands for'. For NEOs, ethics and perspective are vital ingredients in reliability. A daily newspaper has a corporate outlook; while its large resources are capable of extracting information from around the world, its editorial stance filters news to cater for majority interests rather than the more localised, personalised, and individualised issues relevant to NEOs. So skimming daily papers provides a kind of barometer of what's going on in the mainstream world, but the newspaper of today has not yet evolved into a NEO magnet of the future.

The increasing prevalence of independent sources of news and information, including www.crikey.com.au (a daily independent news commentary and analysis) and www.eureka.com.au (a daily independent investment commentary and analysis); blogs; and podcasts that filter news into more specialist topics and perspectives all suggest that such sources can more accurately and efficiently provide for the interests and concerns of individual NEOs.

The Internet enables this demand for multiple sources and myriad specialist perspectives to be met. Sarah Fielding has her homepage configured for several syndicated news feeds that deliver a wide range of topics which interest her — from news, sport, and economics to travel and cooking, and even forward-fashion news and images from www.net-a-porter.com. She buys a newspaper so she can read the business section on her bus to work, but more frequently she simply downloads podcasts onto her iPod on her specific topics of interest. The depth of information available in a podcast from Sarah's favourite commentators and experts, and its direct personal relevance, is more enticing to her than the generalised formats of the daily newspapers.

Reliability is also about timeliness. Once, watching a nightly news programme on television was the authoritative and most up-to-date way of accessing news. In the new millennium, however, television news that is hours or days old is not news at all. The Internet delivers headlines and up-to-the-minute news in real-time and in a more convenient and active format for NEOs, wherever they are and whenever they want it—to an office workstation, a mobile phone (in video, podcast, FM radio, or text format), or a mobile hand-held device.

Television and newspapers must evolve into different news gatherers, offering not old headlines but, rather, the colourful details and in-depth analysis behind the stories on the Internet. Watching the nightly news has become a comforting social habit rather than a mandatory way of staying in touch.

Skimming

With so many sources of information available to NEOs, skimming is the necessary skill of filtering which source and which issue is worthy of the investment of time and effort.

Skimming daily papers provides a kind of barometer of what's going on in the mainstream world. NEOs account for the majority of readers of broadsheet dailies, and during the week are four times more likely to read *The Australian*, and twice as likely as Traditionals to read *The Age* or the *Sydney Morning Herald*. They also account for 64 per cent of the readers of the weekday *Australian Financial Review*.

Few people read the daily paper from cover to cover anymore. The act of skimming is a satisfying way of keeping in touch, not only with the main news and political insights of the day, but also with each of the categories that newspapers package into sections such as arts, entertainment, lifestyle, fashion, motoring, and employment. Many of these sections, developed in the 1980s, have now become redundant or legacy sections, and newspaper editors must either reinvent them to reflect the interests of the NEO leadership or face a very uncertain future.

The combination of free-to-air and pay TV provides a patchwork of perspectives that better represents reliability. NEOs regularly choose to graze across news networks such as the BBC, CNN, ABC, and NPR to decide for themselves what's going on in their world.

Sifting

Sarah Fielding is a loyal customer of her local newsagent. She is a valued customer because, apart from the weekly barrow-load of newspapers she buys, she also has standing orders for weekly and monthly specialist magazines. While she worries about the volume of newsprint that goes in her recycling bin every week, her monthly bill is rarely less than $200 and, given that she travels so much on business, it would probably be cheaper and more convenient for Sarah to use a wider range of suppliers—buying papers and magazines on the way to bus stops, taxi stands, and airports.

Sarah's loyalty to her local newsagent is based on the quality of service it provides. And while the owner of the newsagency isn't aware of it, he is an exemplar for the future of news and information services. Each morning, as the news-papers are sorted for delivery, Bob, the gruff man who helps out with the early shift, separates the sections that Sarah requested and throws the rest away. This way she knows that she won't miss the eating-out section on Tuesday, the invest-ment section on Wednesday, the information-technology section on Thursday, and the arts and entertainment guide on Fridays.

Sarah would like everyone to be able to order only per-sonally relevant sections of the newspaper in this way. After all, since it can be done electronically by her Internet infor-mation sources, she can't see why it's not possible for newspapers to do the same. She'd even pay more to get just what she wanted. She's heard that the technology already exists to sort and deliver newspaper sections and to deliver relevant sections electronically for her to print in a format that suits her.

However, she also knows that corporations move more slowly than NEOs, so until then she is delighted to have created her own version of sectionalising the news and infor-mation she loves. It's her secret with Bob, and they both get satisfaction from breaking the traditional rules about how newspapers are delivered.

NEOs such as Sarah are frequently frustrated that service innovations made possible by the Internet take so long to be translated into the offline world. Consider RSS (the tech-nology that allows customised news items to be delivered to an individual's computer) as a compelling tool for sifting or filtering information. Most NEOs tailor their Yahoo! home pages to have news from a variety of sources and across a range of interests delivered automatically to their desktop as it happens. NEOs' mobile phones sift callers and announce them with different ring tones, and their email programs sift incoming mail into useful mail and spam.

In the vexatious field of direct marketing and direct communications, NEOs want credit-card providers and retailers who send them monthly statements, brochures, and catalogues to use sophisticated analytical tools so that they receive only offers and information that relate to their categories of interest. In other words, they want marketers to stop sending homewares and baby-clothes offers to young male NEOs with a clear pattern of buying music, software, alcohol, and concert tickets. It's even more frustrating for NEOs when they find this kind of smart information being used by a retailer in the USA to send tailored catalogues online, while Australian retailers, where NEOs spend the most are, by sending the same information to everyone, treating NEOs like Traditionals.

Because NEOs are better informed and better connected, and more active spenders, they are also more demanding. These demands are, however, rarely unreasonable or idiosyncratic attitudes; rather, they are the result of NEOs' propensity to sift information on the latest trends and directions from around the world, find something that is worth spending money on, and ask, 'Why can't it be done here? Why can't I buy that here?'

Sharing

Sharing information is a social activity for NEOs. That's why being well informed is so important to them. But equally important is the sense of being inspired, challenged, and connected with other people who share common values and interests. It is here that magazines claim their role in NEOs' lives. Magazines fuel and affirm NEOs' deep desires for beauty, design, and personal evolution. Magazines give in-depth information on specialist topics, they allow NEOs to share in the nuance and detail of an expert's-eye view of a topic, and they provide the high-quality images that capture and display objects and experiences to fuel both imagination and ambition. It is their ability to engage and inspire that makes them so popular with NEOs.

NEOs are twice as likely as Traditionals to purchase magazines from four of the main categories — women's fashion, business and financial, food and entertainment, and information technology and computing.

Newspapers recently came to understand the role of high-quality specialist lifestyle magazines in attracting NEO readers and consequently advertising revenue: as shown for example, by the *Good Weekend* magazine inserted in the Saturday editions of *The Age* and the *Sydney Morning Herald*. These magazines, delivered via NEO-preferred newspapers, create value by delivering the kind of high-quality, colour, in-depth coverage of lifestyle topics that newsprint cannot. Of the 300,000+ readers of the ground-breaking *Australian Financial Review* monthly magazine, 57 per cent are NEOs. In fact, NEOs are a staggering five times more likely than Traditionals to read the *AFR* magazine each month.

More recently, the monthly *Sydney* and *Melbourne* magazines inserted into the *Sydney Morning Herald* and *The Age* have also attracted majority readership from NEOs. A look at their editors provides a vital insight into the NEO dominance of these magazines. The *Sydney* magazine was created under the imaginative leadership of Lisa Hudson, and set the template for its Melbourne cousin some years later. Brook Turner guided the *AFR* magazine to a unique place in the corporate market where beauty and experience were as important as business and expense sheets; where the arts and design were as important as golf and economics. Lisa Hudson and Brook Turner, both quintessential NEOs, created magazines for people like them—more NEOs—and the commercial results are now the stuff of legend.

In the television market, NEOs are almost 20 per cent more likely than the general population to watch commercial television in Sydney, and 12 per cent more likely to do so in Melbourne. And, given that $2.7 billion of advertising revenue is generated by the metropolitan market, and that NEOs spend more and do so more frequently, it makes NEOs the new measure of success for television executives.

However, understanding how to engage with NEOs while they're watching television is not as simple as reaching Traditionals. The conventional wisdom is that television advertising relies on reach and frequency. Reach ensures that a television commercial is seen by as many 'eyeballs' as possible (regardless of their true economic value); frequency ensures the same eyeballs see the commercial a requisite number of times. This approach is fine for Traditionals, but it doesn't respond to the need for engagement, motivation, and action. Viewer involvement and participation in commercials underpins the need to get the creative execution right for NEOs—not just on television, but in every medium.

You don't need to use rocket science to reach NEOs; however, it is essential to use science and special rules to motivate them. That's the key to their economic castle.

Television executives in Australia are slow to learn these lessons, with ratings based on single-definition demographics, and programming strategies designed to attract the largest number of viewers. That is a perfectly suitable measure of success if the prize is measured in terms of which network has the most viewers.

However, if the goal is to achieve revenue, margin, and profitability, this race for the mass market is far from optimal. Traditionals are, after all, half the TV market but represent less than half the value of NEOs. TV executives, therefore, need to attract only half as many NEOs to deliver the same commercial value to advertisers. Or, put another way, every NEO attracted to a television program delivers more than double the value of any other viewer.

Because free-to-air television executives have been so slow to respond to the new consumer dynamic, the impact of the Internet on television has been dramatic. A quarter of all NEOs watch less television as a direct consequence of their use of the Internet. And a quarter of Australian households subscribe to pay television, with NEOs 20 per cent more likely than the rest of the population to be pay TV subscribers. The rise and rise of the Internet and subscription television in Australia has been powered by NEOs. In stark contrast, Traditionals are 9 per cent less likely than the rest of the population to subscribe to pay TV.

While newspapers, TV, and magazines still provide a powerful source of content for NEO conversations, it is Internet and mobile phones that fuel their engagement with the people and interests they care about most.

While 71 per cent of all Australians own or use a mobile phone, 89 per cent of NEOs are mobile, and spend more than the rest of the population on mobile bills and more on high-margin services such as global roaming, Internet access, and sending and receiving messages, pictures, and other multimedia objects including videos and ringtones.

NEOs might sound like the category of technophiles commonly described as early adopters; but, in reality, they adopt new technology only when it offers them a distinct advantage over current technology in delivering better control of their lives. So a new technological feature in itself will not automatically attract NEO attention. However, the added quality and services provided by the new 3G mobile-phone networks has been almost entirely taken up by NEOs. They are ten times more likely than Traditionals to own or use 3G technology.

The *Village Voice*: birth of a NEO newspaper

Frustrated at the paucity of news about her new home suburb of Balmain, smart journalist and new mum Kylie Davis decided at 25 years of age that she would do something about it. As a result, the *Village Voice* newspaper was born. Kylie's own story exemplifies the NEO credo of 'If you need something but find it doesn't exist, go out and create it yourself.' It's also a fascinating insight into the new newspaper.

Kylie Davis had moved up to Sydney from Melbourne and just had a baby. But, as she told us, 'When I looked in my local papers to help me understand my new home, there was nothing in them about where I lived'.

Davis had moved to Balmain in the rapidly gentrifying inner-west of Sydney. Two local newspapers covered her home turf—*The Glebe*, owned by Cumberland, a News Ltd subsidiary, and *The Inner Western Suburbs Courier*, owned by FPC Courier Newspapers.

'Each paper boasted that it covered 45 suburbs or more, yet they had only 13 or so news pages, and each of them with prominent ad ratios.

'It's not about being a journalistic snob. It's about pure and simple maths. You cannot cover a local community intimately when you have only 13 pages of content, and 45 suburbs to spread yourself across.'

A former journalist with *The Australian*, Davis decided to apply her news values and experience to her new patch.

'Hundreds of pages of real estate advertising are not an alternative to local news. Rewritten press releases from major retailers and government bureaucracies putting on a saccharine-sweet gloss are not an alternative to local news,' she declares passionately. 'The idea was so simple, it was beautiful: let's put local news back into a local city newspaper and see what happens.'

What happened next is an example of how NEOs' unmet demand for services often forces them into being entrepreneurs. For Davis, the issues were resolved by asking 'Why can't I?', and then 'Why don't I?'

'The idea to create a newspaper was a great one, but how on earth was I going to do that? I had a seven-month-old baby. We had no money to invest because we'd just renovated our home. How on earth was I going to fund the printing of a tabloid weekly?' she says. The answer to that question was easy. She wasn't.

Rather than be deterred, Davis worked out a way around it. Her paper would be monthly, and it would be A4 in size and printed by the local printer, who she convinced to go into business with her. And once these key decisions were made, the business began to take shape.

'The *Village Voice* was not going to cover 45 suburbs—it was going to cover just one area and cover it well,' says Davis. 'Going monthly meant that we didn't have the sales pressure of a weekly that would force us to look for any business willing to spend quickly on advertising and therefore need to cover a broader area. Going monthly meant we could put some perspective into the news as it affected Balmain and Rozelle. Going monthly meant we had time to visit clients and sell the advertising in a way that built relationships.'

The A4 sizing also had strong advantages. On such a micro sizing, a maximum of three advertisements could be run on a page. As a result, advertisers loved the benefit of not having their sales messages buried under other ads. And being monthly, advertising was affordable. Even the smallest local business could afford the couple of hundred dollars that advertising in the paper cost. That compared favourably to the thousands of dollars per page for the established opposition — and their higher wastage rate.

'The small format and monthly distribution also had benefits editorially,' Davis said. 'It meant that space was limited so we could be really picky about our story list. Generic information was never run. Very quickly, we developed a tag of being 'proudly parochial'. If it didn't happen in Balmain or Rozelle, it didn't happen as far as we were concerned; and while it may have sounded hokey, we made fun of the hokeyness. The journalism was good — it was never amateurish. We were interviewing the mayor and the chairman of a residents group rather than the prime minister or the head of an environmental movement, but the underlying principles of journalism, of fairness, accuracy, balance, and good writing were the same.'

The Balmain and Rozelle *Village Voice* was launched on 1 July 1994. The first edition was 24 pages, and the paper never looked back. The second edition was 32 pages, and it quickly grew to a regular 68 pages. After three months, Kylie Davis bought out her business partner. And, after three years, issues featuring a glossy cover and full colour throughout showed that the publication had arrived.

Davis says the reaction of her competitors was interesting. They ran features and special pricing and promotions to force *Village Voice* to undercut its prices.

'They didn't understand what we were offering, but our readers and our advertisers got it straight away. If you're a newspaper that covers 45 suburbs, you can't focus on one suburb every week or you risk offending the other 44.

'Balmainites understood that what we offered was genuine. The *Village Voice* really wanted to represent the news, issues, and people that locals cared about. My contention was that the harder and faster the world became, the more people wanted to come home and connect back in, but the less time they had to catch up with the gossip over the fence. Each month, therefore, the *Village Voice* gave you the news, information, and gossip that you needed to know to connect to where you live. That was our brand.' And it was a decidedly NEO brand.

The newspaper was able to get underneath its competition and carve out its own market extremely quickly and effectively. 'The short attention spans and inflexibility of the bigger media companies was our greatest ally,' Davis says. 'There was a delicious sense of irony to it. Here I was, someone who had had my news instincts honed by News Ltd, about to set up a newspaper under their radar because they were complacent about their market.'

Within five years, *Village Voice* had totally captured the Balmain and Rozelle retail advertising market from its competitors. The Glebe, Leichhardt, and Annandale *Village Voice* began in 1997, and the Drummoyne, Five Dock, and Concord *Village Voice* was started in 1999 after the company took on shareholders to fund its expansion. During that time, the newspapers trained more than 50 staff in newspaper basics—in particular, journalism and sales cadetships—and Davis says this was one of the most rewarding parts of the business.

'I found my own cadetship at News Ltd a very emotionally exhausting experience and I really wanted my own corporate culture not to have that element in it,' she says. Journalists who emerged from the incubator of the Davis corporate culture have since gone on to work at Reuters in New York, Murdoch Magazines, News Ltd in Australia and the UK, Fairfax, and FPC Courier.

In 2003, after building annual turnover up to more than $1 million, Davis made the decision to sell the *Village Voice* newspapers.

'The aim of the project had always been to sell the newspapers eventually,' she says. 'It was never to create a family empire. Initially, I created the paper to be a job for myself as an editor, but that role changed and grew as the papers developed and expanded.'

The *Village Voice* newspapers were sold to the Tasmanian-based Harris Group in December 2003. Harris had held the printing contract for the previous four years, and helped Davis introduce many technological changes into the business. The newspapers held the record for being the first newspaper in Australia to be printed from a PDF emailed to the printers (at the time, raw PageMaker files would be saved onto a Zip disk and rushed to the airport). But, shortly after that deal, Harris itself was bought by Rural Press, and the combination of a large-scale traditional rural publisher and a vibrant outside-the-box, inner-city newspaper group was not a good fit.

Within six months, both Rural Press and Davis were in agreement that the company should be sold again. It was purchased by FPC Courier—publishers of the *Wentworth Courier*, *Southern Courier*, and their old adversary, *The Inner Western Suburb Courier*. Davis oversaw the merging of the *Village Voice* publishing systems into the FPC Courier framework and then took on project publishing for her new employer before being made editor-in-chief of NSW Suburban Publications.

In eleven years, she had gone from setting up a small local news-sheet under the radar of the big boys to running the editorial team of seven newspapers, and advising her former adversaries on how to create the very editorial content that they had once dismissed as 'too local and micro-marketed to bother with'.

Davis then moved to Fairfax as a senior editorial executive.

'The *Village Voice* was started to show the big publishers that the way they were going with newspapers—of homogenising communities and lumping disparate areas together for the sake of economy—was wrong. We set out to show them that local news didn't have to be rubbish. We set out to show them that people do want to connect to their communities, and that newspapers play a major part in that connection, and that such newspapers can have viable markets if you're prepared to think outside the square in terms of delivery.'

The *Village Voice* was a parable for modern publishing.

'A newspaper is no longer about printing something on paper. A newspaper is now about information delivery. We are a state of mind, an information filter to readers. It doesn't matter whether they are reading us as a broadsheet, as an A4 news-sheet, online, or tabloid—readers connect because of what we stand for journalistically. From there, our ability to attract eyeballs creates an advertising forum and ability to reach out. That's our core being. It's what we are. Newspapers that don't understand that and get hung up on the physicality are operating in the wrong age. Newspapers are no longer essentials like bread and milk. We're an emotional connection.'

10

Food and Wine: NEOs celebrating the good life

Provenance (*Noun:* Place of origin; derivation. Proof of authenticity or of past ownership.)

Innovative Food: the new hunter-gatherers

For Traditionals, food is fuel. For NEOs, you are not only what you eat, but how you eat. Eating and drinking are a conscious celebration of the passage of the day: a tangible demonstration of the good things in life.

The high expectations of NEOs and their wide experiences make them demanding customers of produce markets, grocers, delis, bakeries, and butchers. NEOs dominate the consumption of high-discretionary choice foods, including seafood; free-range poultry, including chemical-free chickens and ducks; and hand-made sourdough breads, bagels, and croissants. And these smaller specialty food retailers would not be in business without the existence of discerning NEOs who are willing to pay a premium for high-quality and luscious experiences and, more importantly, who are willing to overlook the concrete convenience of supermarkets and megamarts to build longstanding relationships with individual businesses that share their passion for food.

The very process of researching, planning, sourcing, and sharing food is an obsession shared by most NEOs, regardless of whether they are confident or even competent cooks. The complexity, diversity, and dynamism of the food available in today's cities create an automatic magnet for NEOs looking for new challenges and discoveries. And as rural and regional Australia recognises that high-quality, authentic food can attract premium NEO travellers, a growing number of opportunities exist for NEOs to celebrate with food outside the big cities.

Since authenticity is emblematic for NEOs (a defining characteristic that drives their high-frequency spending), it is no surprise that NEOs will choose an individual food specialist over a supermarket chain, and a product with strong provenance over a product with strong promotion. NEOs want to know where their local food and produce originates so they can have a strong connection with it, and through the food have a relationship with the people who produced it. NEOs were the first to embrace the Slow Food movement and to use terms like 'food miles' to examine how far an ingredient or product has travelled. If it has travelled more than 50 'food miles', it is treated suspiciously.

NEOs want strong evidence that there is a clear philosophy and vision behind the food and the merchandising. They want to see the passion that makes the food stand for something and worthy of being bought and consumed. They want something that is handmade—the antithesis of the mass-produced—because it signifies individuality, the unexpected, a more intense and unpredictable flavour, and the possibility of a closer match with an individual's sensibility and palate than something produced in response to the generalised needs of the mass market.

Safe and predictable food is unattractive and unappetising

to NEOs. They see 'safe' and 'predictable' are qualities too often used as an excuse by institutionalised food producers and retailers to deliver food that is convenient, and which they produce at low cost and high volumes (and therefore profitably), but are bland and sterile to consume. NEOs want authentic, high-touch ingredients because this brings the assurance of quality as well as unexplored pleasures and possibilities. They want to be challenged by design, new flavours, new information, new combinations of food, and new philosophies like the Slow Food movement and its sustainability credo.

Good food retailers understand that food is more than just fuel or sustenance. Its innate appeal operates also on a sensual level: the way it looks on a shelf creates strong tactile responses; design and style create a level of stimulation and pleasure. Where there is strong and textural design in food retailing, it signals to NEOs that a richer experience lies ahead than that offered by a commoditised, standardised supermarket. It signals that the produce is valued for something more complex than its transactional or functional value. For NEOs, design needs to be valued equally with functionality.

Sarah Fielding is not yet a confident cook. She finds herself regularly caught up in work or social life, so she's rarely at home long enough to plan and prepare a meal for friends. But Sarah loves to eat well and to shop well. She prefers to shop on the way home, choosing a different combination of fresh and ready-to-eat ingredients from the strip of shops near her home. One of the things that most attracted her to her current home is the strip in Potts Point. It has an Italian greengrocer who turns fresh produce unsold at the end of the day into interesting juices, pasta sauces, and soups. There's a Chinese noodle shop that also sells roast duck, chicken, and pork. There's a café that bakes its own bread and cakes. There's an old-style milk bar run by a Lebanese family that has a great selection of cheese and antipasto, and enough basic household items to get her through most weeks.

Once a month, Sarah makes a visit to the supermarket in the sprawling concrete shopping centre nearby. She calls it 'guerrilla shopping', and times how long it takes her from entering the carpark to leaving it; she just wants to get in and out as fast as possible. She would prefer to use online shopping but, unfortunately, lives in a building where the security setup prevents home delivery. When she does make time to cook for friends or family, Sarah plans a special trip to jones the grocer or Simon Johnson. She'll take time to explore the store, stopping to taste, having a coffee, and browsing a cookbook, immersing herself in all the options and possibilities. Then she'll ask one of the foodie shop assistants to help select the ingredients and accessories she needs to turn her inspiration into a celebration. It's always an expensive visit, but Sarah sees it as an investment—in her own skills, in the asset that is her kitchen, and in her most precious experiences.

NEOs expect food retailers not only to know something about the food they sell, but also to value and share an interest in the food for more than its functional value or utility. They luxuriate in the more social aspects of food—its value as a gift, entertainment, indulgence, cultural expression, discovery, or exploration.

In the same way that a bookshelf reveals the personality and values of a reader, the range and quality of ingredients and accessories in a kitchen reveals an understanding of people who value the act of dining, cooking, baking, and celebrating. This applies equally for sellers and for shoppers. The presence of 'adjacencies' in a food store is a vital piece of tangible evidence of these shared values. Adjacencies are items from other categories such as bowls, colanders, cheese graters, pasta machines, and table linen that will be used when someone buys ingredients for a pasta sauce such as fresh, organic basil and vine-ripened, local tomatoes.

Rich information is embodied in food, and NEOs love to know as much as they can about what they eat. They collect stories about ingredients, local producers, specialist sellers, and the different ways that each culture approaches preparation and presentation. Rich information helps NEOs make informed choices about what they eat and how, and where and when they eat it. The better the information, the more intense the consumption arousal.

Cliffy's Food Store at Daylesford in Victoria demonstrates how many of these characteristics can be expressed to attract NEOs from the local area as well as from across the state. Cliffy's was developed by Mary Ellis and Geoffrey Gray who, together, created an atmosphere of eccentric intimacy that evokes a time when food and eating were more central to our daily culture. Housed in one of the town's original stores with period counters and display shelves down each side of a long, high-ceilinged room, taste temptations spill out at every step. In a side-room, there is a café to enjoy the store's produce made into simple yet original meals. It is deliberately anti-urban and also anti-rural—they wanted it to be different from anything available in Melbourne and also different from what people expected to find in Daylesford (a large rural town that has become a destination for spa-goers).

Geoffrey envisioned retail 'theatre' with layer-on-layer of honest, eclectic, riotous, complex, abundant finishes and textures, and Mary brought to the enterprise a powerful commitment to local, regional, seasonal, rare, and scarce produce characterised by the handmade. She sought out, nurtured, and valued local individuals who could grow and produce with passion, patience, heritage, and culture rather than size, speed, homogeneity, and technological specialisation.

It is perfectly obvious to the first-time NEO visitor at the front door what Cliffy's and its people stand for—a heterogeneous celebration of interesting, authentic, seasonal food. Cliffy's has a strategy of using eat-in food in the café to drive the retail sales of fresh food, raw ingredients, and bottled and packaged ready-to-eat produce and homewares. But you won't be able to get tomatoes if tomatoes are not in season. You'll be encouraged to try something else, and to understand why it makes no sense to eat a tomato that has had to travel so far from its natural home that it has lost its flavour and its place in an authentic celebration of life.

What makes Cliffy's such a refreshing experience for NEOs is that it is everything that modern food retailing for the masses isn't. It has deconstructed the role of food purchaser and food seller, and operates on the assumption that everyone is interested in good food and good living. There are no boundaries between kitchen and shop, or between shop and café. It's democratic—staff are always called helpers because 'we're all equal and we're all having a good time'—and customers are forced to explore and experience the offerings for themselves rather than wait for 'permission'. It is unexpected—the front-door squeak has been retained as the 'bell' for an old-fashioned country welcome that forces you to make a connection with the building at the outset. It is unapologetic that things may be hard to find, that tomatoes are not in season, that they don't believe in soy milk, that they didn't get a delivery of their fabulous bread because their baker has taken the day off to go to her niece's wedding. It's eccentric—you can't avoid the large personalities that merge bossiness with caring. All in all, it is unforgettably NEO.

Eating Out: on the edge

NEOs love to eat out. They are more than five times more likely than Traditionals to go to a BYO restaurant, and almost three times more likely to go to a licensed restaurant. They visit pubs and clubs more often; they visit cafes more often. They're more likely to seek out foods from a wide range of countries, and more likely to try a new food if given the opportunity. They take their passion for food into the high street and out to a signature restaurant. They're looking for the same things that they look for in a food retailer: authenticity, design, individuality, information, engagement, and edginess.

Few restaurateurs understand NEOs like the legendary Paul Mathis. Paul has managed to attract and sustain a NEO following over decades and a dozen different eating-out formats without repeating himself. He is the kind of food entrepreneur that NEOs yearn for—constantly changing and challenging diners, and bringing new ideas and new ways of looking at the experience of eating out, but with the same dedication to delivering a great experience for individual diners.

Paul Mathis and his colleagues became famous initially for his restaurants Blue Train at Melbourne's Southgate and Blackbird in Sydney. More recently, Mathis created Chocolate Buddha at Melbourne's Federation Square and Soulmama in the St Kilda Baths precinct. He was responsible for Transport—the 'NEO-Pub' at Federation Square—and the creation of Transit, a signature restaurant in Transport. All are very different creations, yet all share a sustained sense of authenticity and edginess that NEOs cherish.

In all the Mathis venues there exists a sense of culinary discovery beyond commerce; of passionate exploration beyond function. His devotion to organic food was pioneering, and wherever possible he embraces low-energy consumption, natural ventilation, recyclable materials, and an accelerating momentum towards vegetarian menus. At the table, Mathis provides rich information about the suppliers and ingredients he uses, the philosophy or food culture that underpins the experience, and even the process of ordering and eating—whatever will assist his customers enter into the spirit and moment of a great meal.

The most successful NEO restaurants look and feel more like a painting or a beautiful stage set than an architect's model; and, while Mathis involves architects with strong design ideas of their own, his spaces allow the emotional and intellectual space for each individual guest to make the space their own. These spaces, even though many are large, noisy, and crowded, provide a positive backdrop for people with strong attitudes and well-developed values to act out the ritual of eating as celebration.

Successful NEO restaurants around the world are either in edgy villages such as the Mercer Kitchen in New York's SoHo or, if they are in safe environments such as Australian Thai food guru David Thompson's Nahm in London, they challenge the visitor's comfort with menu design, interior design, or new food horizons.

NEO food entrepreneurs, in creating spatial democracy, design kitchens that are deconstructed and brought right into the restaurant, thereby shattering old barriers between cooking and consumption. Mercer Kitchen and David Thompson's Sydney restaurant Sailor's Thai are perfect examples.

They also challenge the boundaries between staff and diners. At Blue Train, staff looked and behaved more like customers. And the range of customers was remarkably democratic in response—at any time of the day there were art students, construction workers, business 'suits', and breast-feeding mums all enjoying the food and the experience in the design reminiscent of a 1960s' taxi café of the inner suburbs. Remarkably, the Blue Train had a kind of neutral ego, and provided both the emotional and physical space in which the customers could act out their own roles on a challenging but not threatening stage. At Chocolate Buddha, Mathis extended the democratisation of dining by offering only communal dining at long tables. At this venue, the first large-scale donburi restaurant in Australia, NEOs not only embraced the 'fast food' aspects of donburi that Japanese have enjoyed for decades, but were also introduced to ordering meals that were delivered as they came out of the kitchen, breaking the pattern of waiting for all meals to arrive at the table before starting.

Marking Milestones: the new wine drinkers

Wine is a significant part of the celebration of a NEO life. As with their search for authentic and individually relevant food, NEOs embrace the complexity and diversity of Australia's wine offerings, and are over-represented in every category of alcohol consumption. They are 50 per cent more likely than Traditionals to drink beer and spirits, and 80 per cent more likely to drink wine. Of the four million NEOs in Australia, three-quarters purchase wine in any four-week period, in contrast to 41 per cent of Traditionals.

As part of the celebration of the good life, NEOs find ways to include wine in most experiences. Home is the most common location for all Aussie drinkers; however, NEOs are much more likely than Traditionals to also consume wine away from home. NEOs like to drink alcohol at events and festivals, at cafés and restaurants, and at the homes of friends and relatives.

NEOs also like to try new wines, and to look for the kind of information that helps them decide on which wines to try. Fifty-two per cent of all the people in Australia who belong to a wine club are NEOs. Wine clubs provide rich information about wine, and NEOs love reading about wine, getting recommendations, and using the imprimatur of medals to help them decide which wine will best satisfy their desire for taste and quality.

Traditionals are attracted to brands that provide them with certainty, and the ultimate example of certainty and a status that attracts a loyal stable of wealthy Traditional buyers is Penfolds' Grange Hermitage. On the other hand, NEOs are more likely to choose brands that represent a complex and idiosyncratic combination of values and interests.

Champagne has always been represented as the iconic drink for celebrations. What has not been so clear is who does most of the celebrating. However, even if the lines between sparkling wine and champagne are blurred by Australian marketers, you can be certain that NEOs are clear about the differences. In the Australian media, champagne is most visible at sporting events being sprayed over other placegetters on the dais. The champagne secret is that most of it is being consumed behind closed doors, with friends and colleagues, as a marker of more personal and everyday events. NEOs are three times more likely to choose sparkling wine than Traditionals, and they account for almost 70 per cent of all French champagne bought in Australia. The top 20 per cent of NEO wine purchasers in Australia buy an average of nine bottles of champagne and 54 bottles of sparkling wine each year.

What is it about champagne and NEOs? Firstly, it's authentic: you can't fake French champagne. The allure of the appellation is its authenticity. You can travel to France and walk the little half-acre of terroir that's been producing a single label of champagne for hundreds of years. In the cellars, you can see and smell the centuries of investment and dedication that have gone into the art and science of champagne-making. On occasion, you can meet the great-great-grandson of the original wine-maker—not only a master in his own right, but also a holder of rare and rarefied knowledge.

Secondly, it's arcane; the inside world of French champagne is full of secrets and protocols and stories. It's protected from the mass market. The great maisons know and practise the ultimate rule of luxury: don't flinch in the face of pressure from the mass market. Anyone fortunate enough to visit Moët et Chandon's Château de Seran at Epernay in France will soon discover that it is not an experience to be bought. The quality of the Dom Perignon served in magnums at lunch is matched by the pleasure of discovering and sharing the many whispered secrets.

Most importantly of all, champagne is archetypal. It is the universal marker of celebration in the Western world. Given that NEOs are the most positive and confident people in the Western world, they choose to mark their progress through the week and the month with positive symbolic acts. NEOs buy champagne to celebrate a business achievement; they buy champagne as a gift for friends who need some cheering up or a little indulging; they buy champagne to start a dinner party with friends as a way of saying 'you're special'; they buy champagne for family gatherings; and they buy champagne by the glass to start a meal as a reward for simply making it to the restaurant. But their consumption is private rather than conspicuous.

The more special the occasion, the more money NEOs spend on champagne: they buy four times more Moët et

Chandon, Veuve Clicquot, and Krug champagne than Tradionals. And the more special the occasion, the more time they spend with a specialist wine-retailer selecting the brand and vintage that will fit the celebration. NEOs know exactly why Madame Clicquot, wife of the founder of one of the great champagne houses, reacted angrily when a visiting Englishman complimented her on the quality of her wine. 'My good man,' she told him, 'we do not make wine here. What you are drinking is nothing less than bottled sunshine.'

Creating Stories, Not Just Shiraz: the new wine-makers

Wine is an important element of the NEO experience, but not all winemakers can see the NEO trees for the forest of corporate competition, branding, and promotions. NEOs love exploring wineries and finding the winemakers behind them. Exploring the views of winemakers and discovering their vineyards offers NEOs more than just a chance to taste a new wine or purchase a familiar favourite. Most vineyards also offer special scenery, authentic local food and produce, and the chance to 'borrow' a sea-change or tree-change life-style, to experience quality design, to meet interesting and engaging people, and to acquire new knowledge and fresh stories.

Montalto, on the Mornington Peninsula in Victoria, started several years ago as a vineyard project for John and Wendy Mitchell, and has since evolved into a complex and sophisticated experience for visitors. The vineyard and olive grove provide a spectacular outlook for diners at its restaurant. There is a cellar door, a piazza for casual eating, and a potager garden and wetland for exploring. Montalto sponsors an annual sculpture prize, and acquires the winning entry for display in its gardens. The Mitchell family believes that their business enables them to share their rare bounty with others—and the continuing development of the property is planned with a spirit of sustainability and a focus on creating a community for like-minded peers.

NEOs can plan a picnic in a remote corner of the vineyard, and have their picnic delivered to them in a charming if eccentric Morris Minor rescued and restored from a corner of John Mitchell's past. Programs or events are changed when they become too programmed or don't reflect the regular customer base. All of this reinforces the fact that individuality is valued, and not volumes of visitors and bus tours.

Sharing Secrets: the new wine-sellers

NEOs love the challenge of navigating the myriad brands and varieties of wine. In Australia there are 3,000 table-wine brands, but the top-100 brands by sales account for 50 per cent of the market. In this storm of choice, NEOs—like everyone else—are also interested in getting the best price for their selections. The difference in NEOs' wine-purchasing behaviour is that, if they have the time and the interest, they will have decided in advance (on taste and quality) on their preferred wine labels, and will then be looking for the best price they can get on them from specialist outlets and megastores.

Wine discounters such as Kemenys do a roaring trade across Australia with their Internet and phone-ordering systems, so NEOs don't need to go out of their way physically if they don't value the concrete slab-and-trolley experience of a volume discounter. Since the Internet is their preferred research tool, it's also a convenient and rich information source for wine reviews, and regional and varietal updates, and only a click away from making an order. As NEOs are 30 times more likely than Traditionals to be comfortable giving their credit-card details on the Internet, ordering wine online is a useful way of making a purchase.

If they're on their way home from work, or out to dinner, or just don't have the storage space for a large wine collection, NEOs will treat their local independent retailer as their personal wine cellar, dropping in several times a week to select for their immediate needs. The value of an independent retailer is in the experience they provide; and if they have correctly identified NEOs as their core market, they will create an experience for NEOs that includes individual attention with personalised, information-rich interactions with knowledgeable staff, an edgy range of wines that provide a high-quality drinking experience, and a different set of choices from the 'top 100' brands that are available in a concrete liquor barn.

It is far more rewarding to discuss investment in wine with an independent seller who is 'betting his business' on his wine choices than to ask a shelf-stacker or a check-out person in a megastore whose future is not dependent on his wine knowledge. And because high-quality conversations with NEOs almost always result in high-margin, high-frequency transactions, independent sellers can build their business on sustainable revenue flows.

The bulk of wine sold in Australia is through supermarkets and supermarket-owned retailers such as Dan Murphy and Liquorland. The giant supermarket groups will increase their domination of liquor retailing in the future; and as they do, they will increase the squeeze on wineries and distributors in the race for the high-volume, low-cost profit model of the supermarket culture. But is the cost of volume success too great for the Australian liquor industry to bear? Is it too high for the corner-store, specialty liquor retailer who knows the names of his NEO customers and tailors his stock to their likes and dislikes, and who may well disappear in this rush to supermarket dominance? Is it too high for the winemakers who care about the beauty and provenance of their wines as they are squeezed on price by executives so seduced by the allure of the checkout that they are blind to the beauty and provenance that actually sells wine?

Many specialty retailers will remain stoically independent and will benefit from the NEO fascination with quality service and relationships based on mutual loyalty. As the giants spread, however, expect the parallel explosion of the online channel as NEOs escape the mediocrity of the supermarket culture for an experience that puts them in control.

11

Shopping: NEOs exploring their identities

Hip Strips and Department Stores

Aged only twenty, Sidney Baevski Myer, the youngest of eleven children, stepped optimistically onto Australian soil in 1899 as the ship from Russia moored in Melbourne. He was poor, spoke no English, had no visa and, working initially from Bendigo in central Victoria, soon set about selling domestic items house to house. He was so poor that he couldn't even afford a horse to cart the heavy retail goods, so he carried them on his back.

Twenty-two years earlier, an already successful Welshman named David Jones had finished refurbishing his George Street department store, and was proudly unveiling to amazed Sydneysiders the city's first hydraulic lift. Jones had started his retailing business in 1838, just fifty years after the founding of the new colony.

By the end of the 1920s, both men had amassed a fortune.

In 1927, Jones opened his grand department store in Elizabeth Street, which remains to this day the flagship of David Jones. He single-handedly moved the hub of Sydney's retailing to Hyde Park.

Myer, who moved from Bendigo to buy an established drapery store in Melbourne's Bourke Street, also bought the adjoining properties and built the first Myer Emporium in Melbourne's retail heartland. And in 1927 he bought Marshall's department store in Adelaide, only to discover the management comfortably ensconced on the very convenient ground floor. He immediately moved them to the top floor and, acting on the advice of his London friend Gordon Selfridge, set about excavating a basement 'for bargains'.

The parallels, and competition, between the two companies have shaped the retail landscape in Australia. Each of the founders has touched the everyday lives of Australians for more than a century. No one living can remember an Australia without David Jones or Myer. They built true fame and fortune on an emporium model of retailing that offered consumers 'everything under one roof'. The emporium model taught Australians how to shop for discretionary goods. But that was then, and this is now. The retail landscape has been forever changed by the emergence of NEOs and their demands for individuality, change, and relevance.

The Sidney Myer emporium model of everything under one roof had become irrelevant by the 1970s when categories of merchandise started exiting the department store. The hardware department at Myer was one of the first to go. Today, stand-alone brands such as Bunnings (hardware), Harvey Norman (electronics and furniture), Borders (books and music), Officeworks (office stationery and equipment), Capt'n Snooze (beds), Ikea (furniture and homewares), and many others do a better job in their various categories outside the walls of the department store. The emporium has lost its status as the one-stop, everything-under-one-roof purveyor of cherished items for a family home.

And while the department stores have, in the intervening

years, been grappling with competitive, financial, and supply problems, the nature of demand has also changed. The consumer landscape has evolved and is driving the department store firmly towards a quality-and-service culture again. NEOs dominate discretionary spending, and it is now the case that a department store lives or dies on discretionary spending rather than basic needs.

Mark McInnes, one of Australia's handful of world-class retailers, devised for David Jones a solid future built around quality and a service culture. His clear strategic choices continue to be supported by the retailer's customer base: more than 70 per cent of David Jones' customers have NEO characteristics. An intuitive understanding of the NEO psychology leads David Jones towards a less crowded store experience, genuine sale events, an expansion of the exclusive designer-brand strategy, and the creation of a quality, often edgier range of merchandise with increased margins per store. The work of Mark McInnes, Stephen Goddard, and Damian Eales has borne fruit for David Jones, leaving the new owners of Myer with a huge gap to close. Comparing the growth of NEOs at each department store brand between 2001 and 2006, Myer suffered a decline in its share of NEOs by 7 per cent, while David Jones increased its NEO market share by 50 per cent over the same period.

NEOs want their discretionary shopping experiences to be more individually relevant, and full of discovery and pleasure. They prefer hip strips to concrete malls because, despite the lack of air-conditioned comfort, the lack of multi-level car parks, and the lack of 'everything under one roof', hip strips provide an organic, authentic, and dynamic cluster of retail experiences.

Since the emporium model collapsed and the shopping mall took on a standardised set of retail chains, the fresh air of the hip strip has provided a point of difference. In a hip strip, the mix of retailers can't be dictated by a single leasing agent keen to minimise risk to his rental-income stream; the number of people who come to shop can't be dictated by the amount of concrete carparks available; and the mix of people on any given day will be unpredictable. This is what NEOs want—not the bland muzak of air-conditioned comfort, but the music of the street.

Conversely the mega-mall of the future will reassure Traditionals who expect the predictability of 'everything under one roof', anchored by convenient parking and basic-needs supermarkets and discount stores. The mall will provide NEOs with an option for basic-needs shopping, but will struggle to be their choice for high-involvement discretionary needs.

The department store of the future will be slimmer and more streamlined, focusing not on everything under one roof, but rather on 'how we look' plus a few fast-moving strands of 'how we live'.

The hip strip will continue to be favoured as a model for NEOs who want to be engaged by something different and daring.

I was Born to Shop: *with people like me*

NEOs love spending money. Or at least, NEOs love to be active, engaged, and involved in the modern world. Because they are more active, more engaged, and wider-ranging than the rest of society, they spend more. And, for many, this also means they shop more. Shopping and spending are the same thing for NEOs: even though many will declare they hate shopping (they mean they hate going to a shopping mall or they hate window-shopping), none of them will tell you they hate spending on the things they are involved with. There are also NEOs who have no qualms about describing themselves as 'born to shop'. These are the NEOs who explore new locations and new stores because each new visit offers the possibility of discovering something new and different.

Shopping (or spending) is not exclusively women's business. Male NEOs spend just as much as their female friends, family members, and colleagues. The key categories in which NEOs spend more than anyone else include personal computers and accessories; computer software; communications equipment (all 2.5 times more); sporting equipment (100 per cent more); and men's accessories (twice as much). All these categories are conventionally classified as 'men's business'.

Urban Australia is the place where pursuing passions and dreams generally leads to spending. NEOs accept this nexus, but make theirs personally relevant: getting the shirt that fits perfectly, that is beautifully made, and has a sense of design or provenance that fits with who they are just now. A shirt must feel good to wear and give pleasure, not only in its sensual form but also in its place in the wearer's life story. After all, it's a part of who one is.

Traditionals fight this nexus, and search instead for a shirt that fits its intended function and costs no more than that function is worth and no more than is necessary. A shirt intended for gardening and garage work need not fit well, nor look particularly good; so for a Traditional it must not cost as much as a shirt for public exposure. After all, it's only a shirt.

Understanding how NEOs shop explains how the fault line in the retail landscape has developed since the 1990s when NEOs first started to flex their economic muscles. The definition of a bargain for a NEO is 'something that is cheaper today than it is going to be tomorrow'. Items and services that are perceived as scarce, valuable, precious, desirable, unique,

or unrepeatable will draw greater demand and price pre-
miums. Wine improves with age, so buying well now will be
repaid by the future experience. Discounts in this context are
mostly irrelevant, and likely to suggest lesser quality or fewer
features which, combined, generally lead to dissatisfying
future experiences.

For Traditionals, a bargain is 'something that is cheaper
today than it was yesterday'. The discount represents a deal,
a win against the odds, a way of gaining more function for
less money. Getting a wine that tastes good now, but which
costs less than the going retail price, provides a true sense of
satisfaction—even if the wine is on special because the retailer
can't sell it.

Satisfying NEO and Traditional shoppers simultaneously
is an almost impossible task. Target is one of the few retail
brands that gets close to attracting equal proportions of economic and social types: 38 per cent of NEOs, 34 per cent of
Evolvers, and 31 per cent of Traditionals. Target's offerings
are positioned to attract Traditionals looking for discretionary
purchases and NEOs looking for basic-needs purchases. On
the face of it, this appears a sensible strategy. However,
Target's success defies the number-one retail rule of the NEO
economy: a retail brand must take a clear position on either
side of the discretionary divide. It must be well positioned on
the discretionary-consumption side like David Jones *or* well
positioned on the basic-needs side like Big W. Only time will
tell if Target can continue to defy demand gravity.

For NEOs the experience of shopping is more important
than the mere transaction. So the simple act of buying bread
at the local bakery can shape the day: will it be a dull transaction to acquire mere sustenance, or will it be an engagingly
aromatic experience involving discussions about wood-fired
baking techniques and hand-milled grains sourced from the

local mill? Shopping is a way of expressing and exploring the self. Items take on a symbolic as well as functional value: a scented candle is a catalyst for self-reflection; its use as a source of light and pleasant aroma is secondary.

NEO urban dwellers are accustomed to a readily available stock of well-designed goods on stylish display in their day-to-day shopping localities. In regional Australia, it is more difficult to find these attributes in either the goods or the merchandising. Where they are found, they will be received with a sigh of relief, and immediate consumption arousal.

Discretionary Divas: *books and coffee*

Books, music, cinema are the discretionary divas of spending. No one could really argue that these experiences are essential. All are available 'free' through publicly funded sources such as libraries, radio, and free-to-air TV stations. Looking at the way NEOs shop for these items, however, shows the stark difference between spending for function and spending for experience.

Some people read to escape, but NEOs read to find themselves. Books take a central place in the psyche of a NEO, and have a unique meaning for each customer. NEOs are more than twice as likely as Traditionals to buy books, and they spend on average 40 per cent more when they do buy. Books provide a benchmark against which NEOs can understand and assess their place in the world and their evolution as individuals.

Good booksellers acknowledge the importance of books in the wider experience of life: books can fuel careers, expand homes; they can even change the outcome of a leisure experience. As one independent bookseller in a popular seaside town put it: 'People see us as part of their holiday—and for better or worse, we can make or break it.'

Good booksellers are also seen by NEOs as experts on realms wider than just biography and fiction. Based on clues drawn from books sold, good retailers can make connections with other retailers in the areas that may become a launch point for other rich experiences for their customers. Good book retailers understand that books are inextricably linked to adjacencies: a cookbook is a direct link to a kitchen or dining experience; a history or biography is a link to a travel experience; a design book is a link to a home renovation or a creative arts experience.

Independent booksellers have a relatively small, constantly changing range of titles compared to the huge list of titles and blockbuster displays of the chain booksellers. The inventory of an independent necessarily reflects changes that are seasonal: they are aligned to local and city events, linked to newspapers' book review sections, and depend on peak selling-seasons such as Christmas. This has the effect of maintaining a connection with the larger world and establishing the bookshop as a source of relevance, stimulation, and challenge.

NEOs prefer the engagement and service authenticity of an independent bookseller to the sanitised sameness of the huge discount chains. Because NEOs know they can buy any book on the planet through the Internet, they don't need to look for a store that has 'everything under one roof'. What they look for is a store that recognises and celebrates their needs and choices, and this is impossible in a discount chain store and rare in one of the generalist bookstore chains.

In January 2003, the global book chain Borders established a major store across the road from Readings in Carlton, an inner-urban neighbourhood that just happens to be NEO-central in Melbourne. Reportedly, when Borders moves into close proximity to an independent anywhere in the world, the smaller store suffers a drop in sales of anything up to 38 per cent, and is often forced to close. Readings, however, suffered a decrease in sales of only 3 per cent in the year after Borders opened its Carlton doors.

One reason is that Readings' co-owner Mark Rubbo is arguably the best book retailer in Australia. Another is that the thousands of NEOs living in Readings' trade area understood that Rubbo's store offered more than just the transaction of buying a book. Borders offer a huge range of books at discounted prices. Readings offers atmosphere, edginess, authenticity, staff with an incredible depth of knowledge of every book category on the shelves, wit, personality, and a commitment to serve and satisfy every customer who walks through the door. The sales assistant at Borders is a cashier; a sales assistant at Readings is a counsellor and intellectual sparring partner.

So, despite the presence of a well-presented, well-lit, wide range of books in Borders, there's no way that NEOs will cross the road to pay half-price for a book in Borders that they'll pay full price for in Readings. NEOs often pay more at Readings than they would pay at Borders only 50 metres away, and any retailer who finds this paradox inexplicable will never understand NEOs.

Traditionals, on the other hand, love going into Borders for the great deals and discounts. They can't understand why anyone would pay full price for the same book across the road at Readings.

Both business models are perfectly valid. One is not better than the other; they just reflect the reality that there are two fundamentally different kinds of consumers walking up and down Lygon Street, and every other street in the developed world.

In addition to buying books and music, going to the

cinema, concerts, and the theatre are activities dominated by NEOs. They are 80 per cent more likely to buy music and cinema products such as DVDs, CDs, and videos, and typically spend 20 per cent more than anyone else when they do. They are five times more likely to go to a live rock or pop concert or to live theatre, and more than twice as likely to go to a blues, jazz, or classical concert. They are three times more likely to see a movie. NEOs want to be engaged and involved with people who share their interests. They don't want to be onlookers. They want these live, unpredictable, cultural experiences, feeding their souls and sharing their interests with people like them. This is the culture of NEOs and the culture of their spending.

The inescapable twin of successful NEO retail culture is NEO café culture.

NEOs are almost twice as likely as Traditionals to drink tea or coffee in a café, so to shop and to sip are twin activities. It's no surprise that the early examples of the blurring between retail and hospitality occurred in bookstores. Allowing buyers to peruse books in a relaxed and refreshing café setting means that not only can customers find the book that suits them best; the longer they're in the store the more likely they are to find another book or DVD or magazine that they can't do without.

12

Financial Services: NEOs facilitating lifestyle decisions

Money makes the world go around, so it's said. It certainly fuels the world of the new economic order, and the more capacity (income) that NEOs have, the greater the difference in their spending behaviour from the rest of society.

Yet at the heart of the definition of a NEO are measures of spending, not of income. Income, like other single-factor demographics, is a poor determinant of consumer attitudes and consumption behaviour. There are many wealthy Australians who have a pathological aversion to spending, and have fat wallets that they like to sit on rather than open. Income and wealth does not correlate with spending propensity, but spending behaviour must be fuelled by income or wealth. The science is in understanding who has the propensity to spend and who doesn't. Traditionals, regardless of their net worth, hate spending money; NEOs, however, consider their income and wealth as fuel for the satisfaction of their deep desires.

So it is that NEOs earn more because they are NEOs; they are not NEOs because they earn more.

Spending choices are facilitated by financial services. Transaction accounts, credit cards, debit cards, store cards, direct-debit arrangements, and bill-pay services are all choices made in the context of spending behaviour. In Australia, Westpac, ANZ, and NAB have the highest proportion of NEOs in their customer base, whereas Traditionals favour the Commonwealth, BankWest, and Suncorp Metway.

Almost twice as many NEOs as Traditionals believe that 'It would be ideal if I could conduct all my banking without ever having to go to a branch.' Once again, the experience is everything for NEOs; they dislike branch-banking experiences that inevitably emphasise volume and transaction over relationship, despite the best intentions of the people who design the layout and processes offered in a banking chamber.

For transactions, the Internet offers so much more than a banking chamber. It is no surprise, therefore, that over the past several years there has been an explosion of Internet usage in the financial-services sector. For example, in 2001 only 8 per cent of adult Australians used the Internet to conduct banking transactions. By 2004 that number had grown to 27 per cent—more than a three-fold increase in just three years.

The increase in Internet banking is even more startling in the case of NEOs: over the five years from 2001 to 2006, the percentage of NEOs using the Internet for banking grew from 29 per cent to 65 per cent. The percentage of Traditionals banking on the Internet grew over the same period to only 12 per cent.

NEOs do as much of their financial activities online as possible. They are five times more likely than Traditionals to use the Internet for banking transactions, six times more likely to pay bills online, and eight times more likely to trade shares online.

NEOs use EFTPOS as a matter of course, writing cheques as rarely as possible, and are seven times more likely to pay for their online purchases with a credit card. Traditionals, on the other hand, prefer to do these tasks the old-fashioned way: they write cheques to pay bills, and sometimes even deliver these cheques to the supplier in person. Their preferred method of payment is cash: Traditionals account for more than two-thirds of all people who pay their bills by cash, whereas NEOs account for only 14 per cent.

The credit-card market has reached maturity in Australia; there was only single-digit growth in the number of people who own a credit card in the five years to 2006. NEOs are 1.6 times more likely than Traditionals to have credit cards: more than three-quarters of NEOs (80 per cent) have cards, compared to less than half (48 per cent) of Traditionals.

NEOs use credit to facilitate their lifestyle, not to fund it. Fifteen per cent of the adult population have credit-card limits of $10,000 or more, but the number is double that for NEOs—30 per cent versus only 9 per cent of Traditionals. Because NEOs are confident about their ability to earn enough to pay off debt and because for many, banking is a low-involvement activity, they are not overly concerned about paying interest on outstanding credit-card balances.

While 11 per cent of the population do not pay off at least one major credit card (known in the industry as revolving), NEOs are 60 per cent more likely to do so—making them particularly attractive to financial-services providers.

Of the major bank's credit cards, Westpac enjoys the biggest NEO differential: 42 per cent of its credit-card customers are NEOs. ANZ is next with 41 per cent, National has 36 per cent, and CBA comes a distant last with 22 per cent. Macquarie Bank (55 per cent) and HSBC (54 per cent) dominate the specialist financial institutions.

The credit-card market is reaching new heights of competitive frenzy in Australia and, like all mature markets, is being defined by the discretionary divide. On one side of the divide are a proliferation of low-fee or no-fee credit cards offering low rates of interest on balance transfers and outstanding future balances. These cards have shattered the conventional link between credit cards as status symbols for successful business people and wealthy individuals with gold, platinum, or black credit cards, and their need to telegraph that success to everyone else. Gold cards are offered as just another option, reduced to a colour choice rather than, as the banking industry calls it, a platform option.

On the other side of the divide are fee-based cards that are piling more and more features into their offers and charging substantial rates of interest. Unfortunately for the cards competing on the high-discretionary-choice side of the market, most have entered the competitive fray with features as their silver bullet. This transactional approach to a relationship forces NEOs into a functional evaluation of like-for-like; pitting one concierge service against another, one points system against another. The end result is that few of the fee-based cards maintain a point of difference for very long. Without a sustainable and trustworthy point of difference being offered to them, NEOs will act just like Traditionals and select the 'best deal'.

13

Cars, Homes, and Investments: NEOs investing in a better future

Home is Where the Loan is

When it comes to making big-ticket purchases, NEOs' strong sense of investment in a better future shines through. Australians generally have a strong sense of entitlement to owning their own home and, because of the tax advantages in owning the most valuable residence they can afford, this is a common investment.

Traditionals, with their strong sense that where one gets to in life is more a matter of luck than planning, prefer to pay down their mortgage and sit on their asset. The physical and emotional solidity of a fully owned house is very reassuring. For NEOs, however, the belief in their own agency—that where one gets to in life is more a matter of planning than of luck—strongly influences their investment decisions.

Remember that, for a NEO, a bargain *is something that is cheaper today than it is going to be tomorrow.* So, typically, a NEO will pay off her home mortgage and immediately use the equity to leverage an additional investment in property or shares, or she will use it to 'trade up' to a more valuable residence. The appetite of NEOs for calculated risks usually pays off—and certainly, in the long boom of the last decade or so, the markets have favoured this type of low-risk taking.

NEOs are more than twice as likely as Traditionals to have a current home mortgage, and more than five times more likely to have an investment-property loan. They are also five times more likely to be considering buying and renting out an investment apartment.

NEOs are great renovators and redecorators, loving the challenge of adding value to a property and reaping the rewards of their creativity and market savvy. They are twice as likely as anyone else in the economy to be intending to make an investment on renovations and extensions.

Insuring for a Rainy Day

For people who love to plan and to take calculated risks, insurance offers an attractive option. While there is very little difference overall in the proportions of Australians who have home-and-contents insurance because it is typically mandated by mortgage providers and packaged by insurance companies, NEOs dominate the higher-margin insurance products known as risk insurance.

NEOs are about 50 per cent more likely to have life and private-health insurance than Traditionals—who believe that, since these catastrophic life events can't be predicted, it is better to do nothing and save the money. But NEOs really break away from the pack when it comes to risk insurance: they are almost three times more likely to have accident and sickness insurance, and more than five times more likely to have income-protection and trauma-recovery insurance.

Traditionals save for a rainy day. NEOs insure for a rainy day.

Investing in markets and bazaars

When it comes to discretionary spending, there's no better excuse to spend than investing in the future. NEOs love the

complexity and challenge of researching and planning investments, sourcing and selecting different types of investments,
and managing and refining their investment portfolios. As a
group, they cover the range of investment types—from
antique rugs to cash-management trusts.

The share market is attractive to NEOs: they choose
Australian equities three times more often, and international
equities five times more often, than Traditionals; and they're
twice as likely to own shares but only 40 per cent more likely
to invest in government bonds.

They are also attracted by aesthetic investments, being ten
times more likely to invest in antique rugs, and nine times
more likely to invest in original paintings. They are four times
more likely to invest in antique jewellery, and precious metals
and stones.

Cars: investment or indulgence?

Despite their urban base, more NEOs drive, and NEOs drive
further than anyone else. A remarkable one-quarter of all
Traditionals, almost two million people, don't drive at all,
while 90 per cent of NEOs drive … and drive and drive and
drive: they are 2.5 times more likely than Traditionals to drive
between 30,000 and 50,000 kilometres each year.

It's hard to determine what drives NEOs' investment in
cars. Certainly, they dominate the group of intending car-
buyers in the luxury and prestige segments of the car market.
Could it be that this is because luxury and prestige cars hold
their resale value better than mass-market cars, and therefore
represent a better investment?

NEOs have an indulgent attitude to their cars. Sexy, fun,
and fast appears to be the perfect NEO recipe: 31 per cent of
NEOs, compared to only 18 per cent of Traditionals, say they
would like a car that handles like a racing car. Unsurprisingly,

male NEOs are more than twice as likely as female NEOs to want a car that handles like a racing car, and NEOs are three times more likely than Traditionals to drive a sports car.

Perhaps they're dreaming of sex, but 18 per cent of NEOs prefer a car that has sex appeal, compared to 12 per cent of the general population and only 8 per cent of Traditionals. The NEO gender difference is reinforced when it comes to sex appeal: almost twice as many male NEOs prefer a sexy car. And if sex doesn't feature, fun does: 24 per cent of NEOs, compared to 12 per cent of Traditionals, say they will only buy a car that is fun to own.

Yet fast and sexy does not automatically translate to a showy exterior. The NEO paradox operates in the car market as well as in other luxury sectors. NEOs want quality, design, and performance in their cars, but they don't want the 'badge' as a status symbol: they prefer a brand or badge that whispers quietly to themselves as individuals rather than one that sends messages to others.

The top NEO car brands in Australia are Mini Cooper, Audi, Lexus, Jaguar, SAAB, Renault, Alfa Romeo, and Fiat. Lexus is the top NEO car in New Zealand, while Mini Cooper also tops the NEO charts in the UK.

When it comes to looking for information about cars, the Internet is again the critical tool. Compared to Traditionals, NEOs are far more likely to use the Internet when they are either investigating new car purchases or just wanting to find out about cars.

14

Luxury: NEOs and the lure of infinite refinement

Hand-made shoes and luggage, and a Louis Vuitton travelling armoire, once defined a well-bred, wealthy gentleman and made a statement about his achievements and his position of authority in his world.

Today's travelling man can still order the hand-made armoire for $50,000 from the Louis Vuitton store in Sydney, but is probably aware of many more options for communicating his individual perspective on his world. He's more likely to be wearing the Louis Vuitton caramel sneakers ($810) while recording travel notes in his Louis Vuitton mini-monogram canvas notebook ($230). Luxury brands have become more accessible as standards of living have risen in economies around the world. The demand for premium lifestyle products and experiences has accelerated. Luxury is grabbing headlines and wallets.

This is the result of a momentous transformation in how spending by consumers in developed economies is understood and how this spending is put into practice by NEO consumers. The transformation redefines luxury from rare and expensive indulgences to everyday treats and rewards; from the exclusive province of the wealthy few to the objects of everyday consumption by the new seekers of quality.

Traditional luxury still exists in the 'heritage' forms of ultra-exclusive apparel and accessories crafted from rare materials by artisans. This is still a significant ingredient in the marketing strategies of the luxury houses that are delighted by the mergence of China and India with new generations of consumers of traditional luxury items. But the unsustainable good fortune of the traditional luxury market lies in the fact that increased sales volume shifts a brand into the mass market, which brings with it more price-based competition, more counterfeiting, and more pressure on artisan production methods—the very things that mitigate against its essential value.

Sustainable economic growth in the luxury market is fuelled by high-margin discretionary consumption; and, as we have seen, NEOs fuel this growth by dominating discretionary spending. It is their search for 'what's next?' that drives this type of spending. It is their desire for intensely personal connections with products, services, and experiences that moves them to the next level in their personal evolution.

These are powerful and idiosyncratic motivations that drive NEOs towards brands whose reputation is based on quality and innovation. It is not surprising that these two ingredients are consistently nominated as the key success-factors for those in the business of luxury.

In the world of NEO Luxury, style is not status; it is a constantly evolving desire. This is not a world of consumers-as-victims, making purchases that are dictated by all-powerful luxury corporations which dictate what, when, and how. Rather, this is a world of consumers who are internally driven to explore, learn, experience, and choose for themselves. Every discretionary choice driven by desire opens up a whole world of purchasing possibilities, but only if a brand can unlock the magic ingredients of the exchange—relationship, experience, information, provenance, design, beauty.

Discretionary choices that are not driven by desire are typically outsourced by NEOs to a broker willing to charge a fee to undertake the legwork on their behalf. This major evolution over the past ten years has led to the creation of high-premium services that free up more time for new luxury experiences.

Sarah Fielding, for example, is envious of her ex-pat colleagues in the energy industry in Singapore and Thailand who can take advantage of the battalions of housekeepers, gardeners, drivers, and cooks who are willing to provide their services at a low cost. Along with her fellow NEOs in Australia, she is ten times more likely than her Traditional colleagues to use personal services such as housecleaners, drycleaners, carwashers, personal trainers, and dog-walkers.

These discretionary-consumption choices free up time and energy for pursuing projects and passions. Sarah does not consider the money she spends on these services as luxuries. It is simply a matter of jettisoning mundane tasks in order to get on with life. NEOs can't imagine why someone would wash their own car, unless they loved their car so much that the act of washing and polishing was deeply therapeutic; and Traditionals can't imagine why someone would pay to have their car washed when they could so clearly do it themselves.

Georgie is happy to spend five or six hours a week cleaning, tidying, washing, and gardening, while never even considering that she should pay someone else to do it. After all, it doesn't take that much time, and she'd rather keep the money herself.

The participants in the NEO luxury market consume constantly, keep exploring, keep changing their nests and their jobs, and pay a premium for a premium lifestyle—in every discretionary category from ice cream to moisturising cream. NEOs place taste and quality well ahead of price and status and, as a consequence, yearn for memorable experiences at the top of every category of consumption—not just at the top end of the whole market where traditional luxury has previously resided. They are responsible for democratising luxury by insisting on its benefits in everyday life, and by rewarding retailers who provide it.

NEOs are twice as likely as Traditionals to make luxury purchases: four times more NEOs spend in excess of $1,000 a month on fashion, and twice as many drive BMWs and Mercedes Benz. The luxury list of NEO consumption is seemingly endless and constantly shifting.

The power of luxury symbols

Traditional luxury—that rarefied world of couture fashion, precious jewels, and the Somerset Maugham suite at the Oriental Hotel in Bangkok—is brand-centric. It cares more about *what* than *who*. It is defined by products and brands that confer reputation or status on the purchaser, and it is as vibrant today as it was in the nineteenth century. In the world of traditional luxury, traditional consumers define themselves by the brands that populate their lives and their homes: they make luxury purchases the milestones of a life well-lived.

Many Traditional consumers are wealthy, but wealth is not the automatic companion of taste and style. So, for Traditionals, prominent prestige brands are shortcuts to certainty: clear ways of demonstrating their success, of creating the right impression, and of claiming an undisputed place in an increasingly uncertain world where the rules of who's 'in' appear to change with dizzying speed.

Heritage, lore, reputation, and timelessness all work together to create the world of traditional luxury. In this traditional world, status is style. The traditional luxury icons are indisputable and immutable.

Traditionals are, however, infrequent spenders regardless of their wealth or income. Income is essential to spending capacity—you must have money to be able to spend it—but the insight that challenges traditional luxury assumptions is that those with money don't automatically have any desire to part with it. And this is where the traditional luxury market finds its fault-line.

Consumers with the values and attitudes that drive their desire for the traditional certainty of 'status is style' also have attitudes that shape their spending behaviour. The bad news for luxury retailers is that the desire to own a Rolex watch, for Traditionals, is based on a straightforward functional evaluation of its value that will generally override their desire to pay a premium. They will search, compare, and negotiate with as many suppliers as they need in order to get the very best deal on their purchase. And then they'll buy one or two and never bother again.

The power of luxury relationships

In the NEO luxury milieu, consumers define themselves not by borrowed status and prestige, but rather by what they know, believe, and desire. Fuelled by this informed yearning, NEO luxury is driven by individuals and their ever-changing understanding of the treasures in the world around them.

In case you missed this example in the Introduction, it is repeated here:

Swiss jeweller Otto Kunsli created in 1980 a matt-black rubber bracelet titled *Gold Makes You Blind*. The bracelet has, under its black rubber exterior, a secret cache of pure gold.

Only the wearer, and those in the know, are aware there is gold beneath the matt rubber. This is inconspicuous consumption in the extreme; this is NEO luxury where symbols and *passwords* outrank the mere objectivity of things. This is the NEO world of whispered secrets.

The traditional luxury market is as robust as ever, but NEO luxury is bringing about a new definition of luxury that has expanded the economic base for luxury retailers and has opened a once-narrow market up to intelligent brand managers across the spectrum. The new economic opportunities will be shaped by the new luxuries: rewards for everyday celebrations such as an achievement, a discovery, a relationship, an experience, or an emotional milestone. These new luxuries are signposts for a new way of living.

Exploring NEO luxury

Exploring what luxury means to NEOs reveals an unexpectedly edgy, dynamic, and personally centred set of concepts. NEO luxury is not just an idea—one end of a spectrum from basic need to discretionary indulgence—but also a market, or a series of markets, for products and services that embody and deliver this idea to NEOs. NEO luxury embraces all that 'traditional' luxury has offered, but gives it a twenty-first century sense of choice, challenge, and discovery. It is more individual, idiosyncratic, and illusory, and has far-reaching implications for marketing and selling. Like other discretionary-consumption categories such as music, entertainment, news and information, and travel, luxury markets in the early twenty-first century are being driven by the individual, not the corporation.

NEOs are not afraid to talk about or practise their pursuit of luxury. They seek out refinement as part of their continuing search for new challenges and rewards. They understand luxury as being at one end of a linear spectrum of what is available in the market: expensive, rare, exclusive, and elite goods and experiences that, by definition, only a few people can access and enjoy at any point in time. More importantly, their descriptions of luxury reveal a stronger individual orientation that defies the linear conventions of the term. For NEOs, luxury is an ever-changing, relational, and idiosyncratic ideal. It is more a philosophy or state of mind than a set of purchase criteria; less about everyone else, and more about the individual's personal development and perspective on life.

The best

English historian Christopher Berry wrote the definitive book on the notion of luxury in modern industrialised society, titled *The Idea of Luxury*. He described the challenge of achieving luxury in a world of consumers who seek out rare and unique indulgences, only to find that others also seek the same things. Luxury is the benchmark of what is best in the market in terms of quality, design, and materials. The idea of 'the best' implicitly acknowledges that there is a wide range of price and quality choices available to consumers, and it places luxury at the upper end of this scale. This scale is defined by others—people who have expertise or resources or status—not by consumers themselves. This kind of luxury is characterised by conspicuous consumption, leaving no doubt to any observer that 'the best' is being consumed. In its extreme form, this kind of luxury is called opulence: a deliberate excess of 'the best'.

NEOs' strong sense of celebration and reward drives them to find the people who are setting benchmarks. In the fine-dining sector, they will want to experience a chef's signature restaurant to develop an understanding of 'the best'. Such a restaurant makes use of fresh, rare ingredients in meals that are produced with expert skill and presented with a strongly defined aesthetic. It has freshly laundered white-linen table-cloths, fresh and exotic flower arrangements, high-quality table settings and stemware, roomy table layouts, and a high ratio of expert staff to diners. It is a place where refinement is built in to the experience, and it is this refinement of the dining experience that makes it attractive to NEOs. They want to experience it, learn from it, develop a relationship with the people who create it. It is also placed at the 'fine' end of the dining spectrum by the reviews and the critiques of food and wine experts; NEOs respect the level of independence, research, and experience embodied in a critic's recommendation. Critiques provide a professional authority that adds an extra dimension to the recommendations of passionate, knowledgeable friends and colleagues.

Another example of indulging in 'the best' is to engage an architect to build your house. Only a small number of people in Australia ever engage an architect because of the arcane uncertainty of the creative process and because of the highly discretionary cost involved. 'The best' may be a house designed by an internationally recognised architect in an inspiring place, constructed with highest-quality, scarce, and personally relevant materials. The labour-intensive, bespoke building processes used by building artisans and the resultant outcome of highly idiosyncratic choices of form and finish also constitute a luxury for NEOs.

Out of reach

When something is out of reach to a NEO it represents a challenge ... and NEOs are driven by challenges. In developed, industrialised economies, where the provision of product choice is a major form of competition amongst suppliers, there is always something more desirable that is available to NEOs. Something is always out of reach. By contrast, scarcity (whether the thing that is desired is difficult to produce or experience, or has almost run out, or has only just become available) has always been the foundation of creating demand in luxury markets, and NEOs understand this kind of 'out of reachness' just as well.

NEOs define luxuries as experiences that appear 'out of reach'. They are desired but not readily accessible. The more out of reach an experience is, the more its luxury value increases. It could be a trip to the Antarctic, or an ascent of Mt Everest, or a seat on a flight to the moon. It can be a fragrance or an outfit that has been custom-designed by invitation from a leading French designer. It could be an object of great beauty crafted from extinct or scarce timber by a traditional artisan.

In an everyday sense, too, NEOs constantly calibrate what is 'in reach' and what lies beyond. So any expenditure on an object of desire that is a magnitude above the current budget or income constraints, whatever level that might be, is also considered a luxury; and experiences or relationships that are out of reach are also luxuries. Becoming a member of a special interest or affiliation group whose membership is determined by elite or arcane criteria would also be considered a luxury in this context.

Personal pampering

Luxury, first and foremost, is a name for a sensual outcome. In the sweeping changes of the eighteenth century, we went from seeing luxury as a moral and political choice (because the consumption of luxuries and not necessities was seen as a threat that would weaken society) to an individual choice in which luxury was seen as motivating individuals to be more productive and successful in order to satisfy their inherent desires.

NEOs, therefore, have an innate social context for their understanding of luxury. And to this they add the levels of refinement that come from practising the art of personal pampering in a world full of personal choices. Personal pampering is a construct for luxury that situates personalised, soothing, relaxing, and pleasurable outcomes at the opposite end of the scale from the hard work, discomfort, and self-sacrifice involved in providing basic needs for oneself and others.

Because NEOs are the architects of their own life outcomes they are motivated to push themselves to take control, look after others, work long hours, take calculated risks, and deny themselves short-term benefits for a longer-term result.

The luxury of personal pampering for NEOs is the contrast to this day-to-day state: being looked after, being the focus of caring attention, indulging in sensual or sensory experiences and high levels of comfort. Obvious ways of personal pampering include a visit to a spa or beautician for a facial or a massage, or even having a beautician or masseur make a home visit. But personal pampering can also include high levels of personal attention in a signature restaurant; using a premium brand of shampoo or skincare; prioritising house renovations around a large ensuite bath; staying at a hotel or resort that has a personal butler service; or buying the services of a personal guide in a holiday destination.

In the wide world, where NEOs spend most of their time and energy 'engaged' with people, ideas, boundaries, and aspirations, their idea of pampering is to allow themselves to stand back from the engagement with the mainstream, and to refresh and re-orient themselves as individuals.

NEOs are much more internally oriented than their group-oriented Traditional cousins: their need is to satisfy internally defined desires such as self-discovery and self-challenge rather than externally defined ones such as status and belonging.

In pursuing authentic and individual lives, NEOs have more choices than ever before—which means there are always more decisions to make about myriad opportunities that are presented in each day, and ever more criteria on the checklist to be considered as they 'write their own tickets'. Their ideas about luxury are a natural contrast to the myriad choices and responsibilities of creating an authentic and individual life: having freedom from constraints, indulging in personal challenge and discovery, and making decisions that purely suit oneself.

Freedom from constraints

NEOs are society's great planners and list-makers. This makes them great achievers and adventurers; but along with taking responsibility for creating a place for oneself in the world (because institutions and governments no longer play this role for individuals) comes responsibility for the choices and decisions that one makes along the way, as well as responsibility for their consequences. NEOs rarely say 'nothing can be done' or shift the blame to someone else. NEOs take responsibility for themselves and their decisions.

Freedom from this responsibility becomes a luxury by contrast. Previous generations fought for more choice, but failed to understand the burden of responsibility that is the natural consequence of self-determination. NEOs revel in the choice that they have, but struggle with the responsibility. NEOs describe this kind of luxury as *not* having financial responsibility (that is, not needing to work), and *not having to* plan or schedule commitments (that is, having the freedom to be spontaneous). Luxury for NEOs means being able to explore other roles and personas, being able to do things that are out of the ordinary, or even just doing nothing at all. Most of all, luxury is being able to 'just be the real me'—not conforming to one's own or others' expectations.

Challenge and discovery

Unlike the pampering of the senses in conventional luxury, this kind of luxury is concerned with constantly seeking and discovering challenges to the senses.

NEOs love challenging themselves to find new levels of refinement. There is a sense of scarcity or rarity in these experiences—perhaps because of the strong belief that they require interactions and relationships with people, and that these authentic experiences are harder to find. These challenges can be new taste sensations created by new techniques, new food cultures, new ingredients, or new physical sensations; or new therapies, sports, and activities. They can be new sights and insights: deliberately getting lost or creating unscheduled time in a foreign city in the hope of having an 'unscripted' experience with new people that will allow the participant to see the world in a new way or to gain new skills and knowledge; or gaining rare or specialised knowledge that is only available through relationships with others.

Or they can be new ways of living, through new homes or living arrangements that 'free' one from previous patterns and constraints. Or they might be new aspirations: this may be a desire for 'game over, next level' because they recognise that the playing field changes constantly, and that with this come new possibilities for discovery.

For me only

Another facet of NEO luxury is the highly localised kind, when NEOs consume products and experiences that let them, as individuals, draw a clear boundary around themselves. This is the luxury of being uninterrupted. It is a singular pleasure, deliberately not shared by even the most intimate of partners, friends, or family members. It is not always planned, but always involves struggle and effort. When achieved, it is fiercely defended.

NEO mothers often describe a deep, hot bath as a celebration for themselves: the door locked against the needs of others, the candles lit, the champagne poured, the perfect book and music selected. Or it could be an experience of commissioning a personal fragrance or piece of bespoke clothing, deliberately choosing something for its idiosyncratic sensual and emotional appeal rather than for its functional benefit.

In NEO luxury, the product becomes a personal signature or talisman representing 'for me only', so idiosyncratic that it can't be shared with anyone else. Some NEOs deliberately schedule personal 'time out' in some part of their annual holiday allowance, either in a remote location without the usual phone 'noise' that sucks them back into the external world or in the form of a specialised course or activity that precludes partners and other family members. Some NEOs immerse themselves in personal collections and hobbies: something that only they can do (or would want to), or that only they as individuals are interested in.

The ultimate NEO luxury in this context is 'a room of one's own': an individual space in a home that has no dual function—that is, not also a bedroom, a study, or a guest room, which can be a blank (as opposed to neutral) canvas for the 'real me' to express themselves in their own time and their own way.

NEO luxury is an integral part of NEO lives. The idea of refinement as an aesthetic as well as a worthy personal challenge pervades all that NEOs do and think. Going beyond the status quo, beyond the boundaries of what is possible, beyond personal achievements and understanding, can be both an individual challenge and an individual reward.

PART THREE
The NEO Trends

In this third and final section we explore the key NEO trends that are driving and shaping our future. We have identified ten trends that we believe are making a significant difference in society. This list is not intended to be exhaustive, but it provides a valuable context for considering a NEO-led future.

-15-

Global is the New Local

Globalism as an ideology or political construct is all but dead. But its near relative, the social and economic framework known as globalisation, continues to thrive.

Canadian philosopher and historian John Ralston Saul said during a 2005 visit to Australia:

> Globalism is dead. Since 1995, we've seen a very serious return of nationalism. Of the nation state. In the Soviet Union, you have the creation of about 25 new nation states, and they are extremely eager to embrace their full existence as nation states in the nineteenth-century sense.
>
> Since 1995 approximately, and certainly since the beginning of the new century, politicians, elected officials, have been getting their courage back. And you could say from '911', politicians realised that they were in charge again.

Globalism rose up to fill the void left by the inexorable decline of the British Empire or Commonwealth and the more dramatic unravelling of the communist bloc. Many national governments saw this as an opportunity to forge new alliances, new voting blocs, new world orders. The European Union was born in the vacuum left behind; while it has continued apace as an economic and immigration integrator, its political success has been unspectacular. Talk of a closer federation of the Americas shows no signs of progress. Asia, with the exception of mainland China and Hong Kong, shows no sign of re-aggregating. And in the Pacific, small countries continue to value their own nationhood rather than post-colonial integration with their bigger brothers. Political independence and autonomy have become the bedfellows of economic inter-dependence.

Globalisation, that economic parallel to globalism, has been more successful, aided in no small part by the advent in the early 1990s of the Information Age and the emergence of global-roaming NEOs. Today, managing or conducting a business in New York or London is no different to working in Sydney or Melbourne. Managers have been educated in the global universities, speak the same management language, and are fully interchangeable. An Australian management consultant educated at a Sydney university can effortlessly transport herself to San Francisco or Edinburgh and behave professionally as if she had worked there her whole life. And the time differences around the world, rather than posing threats to seamless workflows, create unique opportunities in a commercial world without boundaries.

Similarly, a NEO in an architectural practice in New York City sends a design-rendering job to India as he leaves the office for the day. When he returns the next morning, the job is finished and waiting in his computer in-box. No matter that it also costs one-tenth of what would be charged in NYC; the importance of business globalisation is that distance now defies the tyranny of the clock. Work is done for us while we sleep.

Because the cost of digital communication is close to zero, tasks that can be standardised and automated will inevitably migrate to the most productive source which, for English-speakers, will be India—expected by 2010 to be the largest English-speaking country in the world.

And it's not just English-speaking countries that enjoy this global benefit. Information-technology specialists in London are increasingly using Bulgarian and Albanian technicians prepared to work longer shifts during unfriendly hours to solve programming glitches in London-based corporations' IT systems. The Bulgarians are not necessarily paid less than their British counterparts. What makes them attractive, however, is their willingness to do work that the Brits are reluctant to do—at least in the required timeframe. What is remarkable about this insight into the future is not that someone from another country will work for less, or work harder; we have all become used to that. What is remarkable is that this is not labouring on a building site or driving a taxi; this is highly skilled, extremely complex computer programming that affects millions of lives if, for instance, a telephone system isn't reprogrammed overnight.

It is therefore the globalisation of education that emerges as one of the major drivers of the future, ushering in a world in which national boundaries, cultural differences, diverse languages, and different cultures are no barrier. It has ever been thus in the arts, such as when ballet dancers educated in Russia filled roles with London's Royal Ballet in the 1930s; or the music of a 17th-century German composer was played in the 1950s by a New Zealand orchestra with a lead violinist from France. Management education has lagged behind arts education in this instance, but globalisation has been with us for almost a century—we just weren't sure what to call it before the economists got hold of it.

Politically and socially, however, globalism is in reversal. John Ralston Saul got that part right.

The integration of business, management, and creativity across the world is, paradoxically, creating not a global economic behemoth but instead millions of local cells linked by economic advantage. Take the example of the New York architectural firm sending its rendering job to India. The artists in Delhi are happy to live where they do. They have no desire to live abroad in one of the most expensive cities in the world. In this newly integrated world they can be found and commissioned over the Internet, do the rendering work in their home studio with their families around them, and earn US dollars to spend locally in their own community. The new globalisation is localisation.

In the unskilled market the result is no different. Take the increasingly ubiquitous call centre, as an example. The US-based hotel chain Starwood Group outsources its call-centre work to a company in Dublin. If you call the 1800 number from Melbourne to book a stay at the Westin Hotel in Sydney you will most likely be answered in an unmistakeably Irish lilt by a relatively unskilled worker who works and still lives with his parents in his home town of Dublin.

While it is naïve to suggest that this outsourcing trend has nothing to do with economic advantage, cost is becoming less of an issue as businesses of all sizes — from global brands to small architectural firms — discover the time-zone, skill, and productivity advantages they gain from using offshore workers. And those global brands that do attempt to behave in predatory ways are frequently exposed by the new ethical examiners who have sprung up in every culture and every sphere of activity. Nowadays, for example, global manufacturers of sneakers or high-end fashion brands who try to use low-cost sweatshops in Third World countries, in contravention of new standards of acceptable ethical behaviour, are exposed and boycotted for their poor corporate citizenship.

And it's not corporate regulators doing the exposing; at least, not in the first instance. It's the new ethicists who were activated by the introduction of economic globalisation. NEOs have become the ethical traffic-cops in the globalised world.

It seems that, as brands became global, consciences became local.

So what we see as this global world develops is a massive matrix of communities of mutual interest growing up across the globe. Most are symbiotic; some are predatory; but all are redefining how we behave as global citizens. And the new definition of a global citizen is 'a person who works on the world stage from a local base'. Global is the new local.

Driving this global trend are intensely individualised NEOs. They are the small entrepreneurs who create enough visibility to be located on the horizon by a New York firm of architects; they are the medium-sized entrepreneurs who have the imagination to establish a call centre in Dublin; they are the global managers who understand the value in employing Bulgarians in London for two weeks to solve the insoluble; they are the new ethicists who expose the behaviour of global bandits committed only to profit at the expense of this new global symbiosis.

They are also the knowledge-workers in new workplaces across the globe: connected, cooperative, everywhere, all the time. The clues for what globalised work looks like for NEOs cannot be found in the large office towers in our capital cities, even though NEOs unhappily dominate those spaces. The buildings that accommodate Australia's global corporations and organisations also house the least productive spaces—because they run on institutional time and false assumptions about how human endeavour is managed, and how a personal best is produced.

Conversely, the most productive and satisfying spaces are

those that do not try to accommodate most of the people most of the time. They are spaces that serve individuals and groups according to their idiosyncratic rhythms. Frequently, they are not traditional workspaces at all. They are cafes, homes, shared think-spaces and, increasingly, planes and a new breed of airport lounge.

The one-size-fits all workspace is already an anachronism. In the same way that there is no longer a consumer middle market—one that tries to be all things to the majority of people—there is also no longer a middle workplace. A company as large as Telstra or National Australia Bank, with more than 20,000 employees, is the organisational equivalent of a whole nation, containing distinctly different subcultures and communities. Conventionally, these work subcultures have been explained in terms of job types: blue-collar field workers are different from white-collar IT workers. But it's patently obvious that all IT workers are not the same: they don't think the same way, process information the same way, or perform tasks in the same way, even if they share the same job type. This is the maxim of the NEO economy.

In a globalised world with local purpose, understanding why and how people engage in the work they do is more important for the future than the work they do. Motivating and retaining people will be more important in the next decade than hiring them.

Traditional corporations still express surprise at these unsettling trends, but their dismay is disingenuous. After all, by putting shareholder interests front and centre, and by making employment just another rational and objective business process to be transacted, costed, and reduced in the name of shareholder value, they are responsible for breaking the emotional ties that link employees to them in a symbiotic relationship of equals.

Artistry, insight, deep knowledge, and unique experiences can't be automated. And these, the factors of competitive global advantage, are highly individual, coming as they do in singular human packages. Smart employers are valuing the NEOs who use their skill and expertise to add value to the bottom line. This is the future trend in a globalised world of international competition for skills. It will fall to the prized NEO workers to choose whether or not to share their knowledge with an employer by creating a relationship based on mutuality, motivation, stimulation, collaboration, and inspiration.

The secret to success in the globalised workplace of the future is to understand what makes people different rather than what makes them the same. And to understand this we need to understand what stimulates and motivates them; what moves them to express themselves. These are the discretionary aspects of our lives—no longer the basic needs. In the world of work, this is what will shape our future. And who better than NEOs to lead the way, with their well-developed discretionary decision-making abilities?

So where is the work of the global future happening? It's happening in micro-worlds, tiny local groups of globally interconnected, specialist enterprises that can move faster, think more independently and creatively, and produce better-quality outcomes than do the leviathan national and multi-national corporates and the mega-departments of our public institutions. It is estimated that up to five million Americans, and more than 50,000 Britons, make a significant part of their income from trading and doing business online. These businesses are fuelled by the Internet, which connects people and tasks more easily than most internal knowledge systems in large companies. The architectural firm in New York City working with illustrators in India is a good example of this trend.

Another example of global being the new local can be found on that icon of a globalised world, the Web. The arrival online of *local search* is transforming how we individually manage our lives. Local search is confined to a single city or even a local neighbourhood. It helps us find a plumber in our locality of interest — which might be where we live, where we have an investment property or holiday home, or where our widowed mother lives.

The traditional system is controlled by technicians, known as webmasters, who decide what information appears, or by advertisers using media such as the Yellow Pages.

Increasingly, however, local search sites are emerging that are controlled, not by web masters or advertisers, but by other consumers, just like us, with widowed mothers. After all, if you now live in San Francisco and your mother with the leaking tap lives in Brisbane, you will be more interested in the opinion of a neighbour from her suburb than a computer technician living in Sydney when it comes to finding a plumber to fix her tap.

Local search will become even more powerful when NEOs integrate it with their mobile phones, iPods, Blackberrys, or other hand-held computers, and use it to find them and either give them the location of the nearest petrol station, or forward emails, or pick up that talking book at the passage they were listening to before they left home.

The world has never before been more global, or more seamless. It touches every aspect of our lives. But as globalisation spreads even further, we are becoming more and more local.

Global is the new local.

The Doctor is in — and it's You

In the Gospel according to Luke, Jesus said he wanted to hear uttered the proverb, 'Physician, heal thyself.' It may have taken us a couple of millennia, but we appear to have finally got the message. In a major trend, we are becoming our own physicians and experiencing the age of self-actuated wellness and wellbeing.

NEOs have never been so aware of the determinants of health and, as architects of their own life outcomes, they have never before been so active in taking responsibility for their own health. While health systems in Australia struggle under the pressure of increasing demand and inadequate or poorly timed and coordinated health services, NEOs are not expecting any government to create a solution for them. They're taking control of and responsibility for their own health, and this will create radical change in future.

The authority of the system's gatekeepers is waning in the day-to-day lives of NEOs, who are frustrated with long waits at GPs' surgeries, pathology clinics, and specialists' appointments, and are even more frustrated by the uncoordinated, incomplete, and barely useful diagnostic information given to them by health professionals.

NEOs need to be in control, but don't necessarily need to

be the 'expert'. They want good-quality information that helps them make their own decisions. For example, chasing all the pieces in the jigsaw puzzle of treatments for common conditions such as migraine, endometriosis, or allergic reactions largely falls to patients. GPs don't have the time, and specialists don't have the inclination, to talk about alternatives, options, case studies, and comparisons that NEOs are accustomed to having at their fingertips for the other important decisions they make in their lives. When this kind of information roadblock occurs, NEOs typically turn to the Internet to fill the information vacuum. In parallel to the demand by NEOs for self-determinism based on rich information, and in an attempt to fill the void left by an out-of-date medical information system, websites are proliferating with social network and decision-support networks such as health-insite.gov.au, a health information site that is not controlled by doctors or their marketing associations; or bbc.co.uk/health, a site with an encyclopaedic menu of health conditions, and their symptoms and treatments.

Personal electronic devices that take the guesswork out of monitoring temperature, blood sugar, and blood pressure are now commonly available, and are increasingly becoming the automatic choice for NEOs, who believe in more information and control, not less. It's even possible to purchase a personal cardiac-arrest machine, complete with audio instructions that adapt the step-by-step treatment process in response to the feedback from the user—including whether or not to administer an electric shock to restart the heart.

NEOs are looking for more personalised, precise, complete, and holistic health services that help them feel as if they are in charge of their health—in the same way that they have embraced health resorts and personal trainers in the last decade. Many will be willing to pay $1500 for a comprehensive, multi-disciplinary health screen each year, rather than $50 for a quick check-up at the GP.

However, wellness extends well beyond medical diagnosis and treatment; it is increasingly entering the preventative world of healthy food and organic remedies.

It is rare to find a NEO who is not interested in food. The aesthetics, the experience, the provenance, and the sensual pleasure of eating all rank highly for NEOs. In the near future, the preventative and curative powers of local, seasonal, and organic food will become more and more important. Conversely, as NEOs become more aware of the enormous distances that food travels between grower and consumer, they will feel reduced confidence that the food available from traditional retailers such as supermarkets will have any nutritional benefit left at all. This is one reason that NEOs are demanding local, authentic, chemical free, seasonal, hand-processed food products that travel very few 'food miles'. A few examples are raw-milk cheeses, perfect veal, organic chicken, vine-ripened tomatoes (as distinct from environmentally controlled truss tomatoes), wood-fired sourdough breads, ripe-harvested stone fruit, and bio-dynamic, free-range eggs.

This wish-list reflects the preparedness by NEOs to forego convenience for sustainability and authenticity. Mangoes ripen in summer, so NEOs don't want imported mangoes in winter. It's not natural. And while some chefs complain that they can't get the white meat veal in Australia they can get in Europe, what isn't disclosed is that to achieve really white veal, the baby animals have to be deprived of iron in their diet and sunshine in their lives. In Australia, vealers from producers such as White Rocks might have a disturbingly short life, but it's happier because their diet is 98 per cent warmed fresh full-cream milk and 2 per cent rolled barley and lupin for roughage. The meat from White Rocks is also hormone-free.

Commercial chickens are bred and reared to produce optimal weight at only nine weeks of age. This is such an unnatural process that they often fall ill; then, as a consequence of commercial imperatives outranking nature, they are fed antibiotics to prevent disease. Saskia Beer, by contrast, grows some of her Barossa chickens out to 16 weeks, and provides fortunate customers with a flavour that is incomparable to 'factory' chicken meat.

The reclaiming by NEOs of responsibility for their own health corresponds to this recent rise in demand for organic fresh food, dry goods, and prepared goods. Demand will continue to rise as the organic food production movement gains critical mass and wider acceptance as an alternative.

Organic, seasonal, and local produce is still mostly a discretionary choice, more expensive and more time-consuming to source and select; but, just as NEOs are becoming their own physicians, they are also driving the growth of the $300m+ organic food industry in Australia. NEOs are 25 per cent more likely than anyone else in the population to buy and eat organic food. In response to this major trend towards organic, Pierce Cody, founder of Cody Outdoor, and Brett Blundy, founder of Sanity Music and Bras N Things, have bought and expanded a range of organic retail stores across Australia. Known as Macro Wholefoods Markets, the stores are often as big as traditional supermarkets, and they offer customers a wide range of organic products and services, including an organic café; organic fruit and vegetables; organic and natural grocery products; organic pet food; an environmentally friendly cleaning range; in-store consulting naturopaths; a natural dispensary with herbals and homoeopathics; natural body and health care; organic wine, beer, and spirits; organic eggs, milk, bread, and butter; and an organic poultry and meat range. At their Bondi Junction store they even offer yoga classes.

As NEOs' appetite for healthy products grows, this mainstreaming of organic products is accelerating at a staggering 30 per cent each year in Australia. However, the focus on health goes well beyond the organic world.

In recent years, there's been much talk of green offices, following on from the debate about sick buildings in the late 1990s. The CSIRO has estimated that daily exposure to toxins emitted from indoor products such as building materials, office furniture, and paints generates costs of up to $12 billion a year due to ill health and lost production. Pollution outdoors is a common concern in capital cities, but indoor pollution has been found to be as much as five to ten times higher than outside levels, and is a growing problem in buildings across Australia. For the average Australian office-worker, more than 40 per cent of waking hours are spent in the office.

CSIRO principal research scientist Stephen Brown is reported as saying that up to 60 per cent of workers in toxic-office buildings suffer from symptoms such as headaches, lethargy, nausea, and eye, throat, and skin irritations, compared with only 10 to 15 per cent of the general population at any one time.

However, there are a few shining examples of intelligent development. Morgan Stanley's Sydney office has, for example, been awarded a five-star certification rating by the Green Building Council of Australia, with one of the award scores based on the fact that 60 per cent of the workspaces had external views. For NEOs, who value human scale, fresh air, and the stimulation of the world around them, and who are increasingly feeling that they have to take responsibility for their own health, the office environment is becoming an important factor in their selection of a work place and an employer. The fight for the desk by the window will no longer be based on one's status, but on one's assessment of a personal health risk.

In the late-20th and early-21st centuries, corporations developed campus models for the workplace that were intended to be more like universities, with horizontal networks of self-organising teams, rather than vertical hierarchies of management layers. Hot desking and so-called hoteling approaches broke the 'my space' thinking, as executives and workers alike were allocated workspaces and resources on a daily or weekly basis by a concierge. This new ideology made sense as a workspace model where shared goals existed between employees and employers in large organisations. However, while the new styles of office buildings were being constructed, and managers were being dragged into an open-plan, desk-sharing environment, the world moved on. Those campuses that were once exemplars of new democratic workspaces were soon exposed as white-collar factories with no more democracy than the exclusive executive washroom of the 20th century. The campus model was corporatised and digitised, and people were again treated as transactions rather than independent contributors to a higher purpose.

It appears therefore that, with few exceptions, it is impossible to create a workspace environment in a concrete tower that genuinely reflects the needs and aspirations of imaginative, creative, team-building NEOs. It's probably more productive for an urban NEO to stay at home, make a coffee on her own espresso machine, and conduct a videoconference using Skype with the other people in her team, rather than to spend an hour in peak-hour traffic breathing toxic particulates, only to arrive at a polluted workplace filled with the anxieties and stresses of independent thinkers forced to work in the modern equivalent of a 20th-century assembly line.

So the new models in this trend towards self-actualising and workplace health will be a blend of what's best in bricks and mortar and what's best in the digital world. And what's best for the individual. Home offices are well-established as a work environment for small enterprises; now, serviced-office providers such as Regus and ServCorp provide a global-office network in CBD locations for people who want to rent office space in a large building, but want to access it when and where they chose: just like renting a hotel room. Regus, appealing to refugees from the large office, use as one of their main marketing tools a postcard with a view from 'your' desk, offered to 100 per cent of users. For example, the Regus facility in Sydney's Darling Park occupies the entire twentieth and twenty-first floors of the new thirty-five storey building, and offers its own courtyard garden and views onto Darling Harbour and the city skyline.

Despite the rare examples of successful office towers, which include Westpac's in Sydney and NAB's in Melbourne's Docklands, future demand will be more directed to micro-office hubs, in which all the benefits of large office infrastructures will be available to direct employees, contractors, and small-business people, and to the 'road warriors' who can't rely on home spaces and want to be part of a work community on a regular basis. These micro versions of the corporate serviced office will be found outside the CBD in attractive neighbourhoods and sea-change locations. Equipped with meeting spaces, high-quality communications and production facilities, and a variety of specialised work-spaces, the distinguishing driver for these businesses will be their ability to create and support relationships *between* users, as well as *for* users and their employers or clients. It will have facilities that are both open to the public and exclusively for the use of customers (like video-conference facilities, in-house 24/7 technical support, business coaches, accountants, and lawyers). It will also offer services that support important family responsibilities, including facilities for working people and for children or older family members, or perhaps even the office dog. It will ideally be located in a NEO neighbourhood, so that workers can easily shop for food and personal services (such as dry-cleaning and shoe repairs) while maintaining contact with their business community.

The micro-office hub and the management ideology that fuel it will be healthier and will, therefore, attract NEOs intent on improving the ways they live their lives. Design will be bioharmonic; construction will be of low-emission building materials rated as totally safe to humans; it will deliver thermal comfort, optimal light intensity, optimal humidity, excellent acoustics, human-safe noise, and thermal insulation; it will offer microbial controls on all air conditioning to remove all bacteria and toxic particulates from the air; it will offer immediate fresh air in garden environments; and it will lower stress by individuals being in control of where and how they work.

It's not just the office that is a factor, but also exposure to other work environments. For NEOs whose jobs require them to travel by air, company policies requiring economy-air travel at either end of a long work day may find that the physical toll of restrictive seating, de-humidified and recycled air, and close proximity to people with infectious ailments is too great a price to pay for an interesting job. In future, environmental-impact factors will gain weight as attractive, stimulating careers are found in smaller, more personalised, more aware, and healthier workplaces. Employers increasingly understand that the health of employees is essential to a sustainable future for the organisation.

In the workplace, at home, and while travelling, NEOs are becoming their own doctors. They will cure themselves by moving to employers, health providers, retailers, airlines, buildings, houses, and lifestyles that not only symbolise the value of a healthy life, but actually deliver it.

The doctor is in—and it's you.

-17-

No-Age is the Best Age

Life stages and age milestones have long been considered indicators of likely human behaviour. When you turned 65, for example, you were expected to retire. When you were in your thirties you were expected to be in the growth trajectory of a career heading towards leadership at 50, or you were out of the workforce having children.

All that has changed, and the transformation is accelerating as age becomes unimportant. In this changed world we hear that 60 is the new 50, but it isn't. Sixty is the new No-Age. Age is now irrelevant.

In truth, age has never really mattered much. Forget the gen Y, gen X, and baby-boomer swindle that makes us believe that all people of a certain age behave in ways that are similar. When you are 20 you are either smart, ambitious, and successful or you aren't. It has nothing to do with being 20. When you turn 60 you are either starting the next phase of a remarkable career or you're retiring. Age counts for zip. And that has never been more true than in the new millennium.

Take, as an example, Mark McInnes, who ascended to the CEO role at the David Jones department-store chain as a 30-something. In just a few years, he took David Jones to a leadership position in the very competitive Australian department-store market. He achieved record sales, record profits, and a record share price—the magical and elusive trifecta. McInnes is arguably the best retailer in Australia, but it has nothing to do with his age; he's just brilliant at what he does.

Or take Michael Zifcak who, at the age of 83, retired in 2001 as the managing director of the Collins chain of book-stores. Zifcak had been employed at Collins for 50 years, and in the last ten years of his career was at the height of his game with 70 stores across Australia under his management. Within four years of his retirement, however, Collins descended into serious financial difficulty and, after 83 years of continuous operation, went into voluntary administration. According to all the age precepts, Michael Zifcak should have been almost two decades past conventional retirement age by the time he finally closed his own personal book on Collins. Yet, so out-standing had been his leadership that, without him, the company failed.

Mark McInnes, in his thirties, is remarkable. Michael Zifcak, in his eighties, is remarkable. They are both exem-plars of the No-Age era.

While age has never really mattered, it is the NEO phe-nomenon that brings the No-Age era into stark relief. NEOs, in psychological terms, are self-actualisers whose internal drive is to go beyond physical comfort and material acquisi-tion towards a deep understanding and satisfaction with the meaning of their own contribution to and place in the world. They do this by seeking out and acquiring what the celebrated American psychologist Abraham Maslow called 'peak experiences'.

Peak experiences are the episodes that signpost a life richly lived. And they have nothing to do with age. Peak expe-riences take place throughout a NEO's lifetime. NEOs are not comfortable with being classified by a single dimension or label such as age; they see life as a continuum, and resist all efforts to assign age-labels to people and their experiences.

For example, in reinventing the ways they live, work, and play, NEOs view work not as a job to be done to fuel vastly more desirable leisure pursuits but, rather, as a new kind of desirable pursuit in itself. It is no surprise, therefore, to observe that 82 per cent of NEOs are in full-time employment compared to only half of non-NEOs. Conversely, less than one in five NEOs are unemployed, while half of all non-NEOs class themselves as unemployed. In redefining work, many NEOs are choosing to be self-employed, and are three times more likely than non-NEOs to work from home — regardless of their age. The work choices they make are driven by desires and inner-directed ambitions rather than any sense of conformity to this or that life stage.

And because NEOs don't view work as a chore, they are significantly less likely than anyone else in Australian society to retire. For every four non-NEOs who retire, only one NEO does. Older NEOs will gravitate to activities that can deliver peak experiences to themselves and well-evolved expertise to others. These activities will involve skills that make direct use of the right-brain — the hemisphere that becomes dominant in later life — including counselling, humouring, supporting, tending, arranging, performing, consulting, educating, influencing, proposing, composing, designing, and writing.

So, while NEOs don't like to retire and don't like to call it that when they do, when they eventually do scale-down their work lives, where and how will they live? NEOs are likely to resist any idea of community living that bestows the stigma of an age-based label, so what will their new kind of residence look like? One thing is certain: they are not heading for a traditional retirement village.

What NEOs want is an environment where they can continue to have peak experiences, regardless of their age and regardless of their physical capacity. They want a No-Age neighbourhood, a peak-experience village. The challenge, and financial opportunity, for architects, developers, and service-providers therefore is to give NEOs the psychological stimulus of being able to choose from a menu of options that delivers more peak experiences—not fewer ones.

Conventional retirement-home developments already come in varied forms. Most are basic institutional boxes or compact versions of conventional suburbs. Others are 'upmarket' medium-density residential developments that look just like their non-retirement cousins, but have a few age-based facilities like wheelchair-friendly designs, panic buttons for medical emergencies, and higher levels of onsite staffing and community facilities such as gyms, group-entertainment areas, and more active landscaping and garden maintenance.

Adding incremental value has been the model used to date, creating slightly more amenity based on traditional, age-related assumptions. This is a strategy that works for the current crop of developers and for Traditional retirees. It will become less viable in future, given that competition on function, features, and price (offerings valued by Traditionals) only delivers low margins to developers.

Creating peak-experience communities or Peak Villages represents the No-Age challenge and opportunity for developers and service-providers. It's a challenge because it's unlikely that any design for peak experiences can be retrofitted into the existing Traditional development template, and because it's unlikely that NEOs will be willing to enter into the narrow set of financial arrangements offered by most retirement developments. And it's an opportunity because those developers who have the imagination to create Peak Villages for NEOs will be rewarded with financial partners rather than traditional customers, higher financial returns on their initial investment, and a significantly better yield on the project as a whole. As we've seen, NEOs dominate discretionary spending. By definition, they have a greater spending capacity and willingness to spend on or invest in experiences that enable them to feel and behave in decidedly NEO ways, rather than being forced into the Traditional channels they so dislike.

It has been established scientifically that NEOs are more likely than non-NEOs to pay a premium for a premium or peak experience. So the new retirement village will need to be a fresh concept, grounded in experience not function, based more on the No-Age individual than on old ideas about what suits the life-stage cohort.

Let's not start with bricks and mortar. Let's instead look at the concept through the eyes of a NEO couple in their sixties who, as great planners and information junkies, want to be in control of the next part of their lives. They are unlikely to consider a move to a suburban lifestyle if they love inner-city life. Wherever they live they will have established satisfying relationships with the Italian butcher, the sourdough baker, the French patissier, the organic fruit-seller, the imaginative and responsive bookseller and, of course, the local restaurateurs. They don't want to downsize simply because their children have left home; they value their space and their ability to have rooms for escape, discovery, and reflection. So they will either convert those extra bedrooms into personal spaces—a home office, a yoga and health room, a room for creative work—or they will look around in the vain hope that a developer has finally understood their needs and created a Peak Village. They're not even thinking of retirement or planning to 'fill in' time. They're planning on more fully exploiting it.

When they consider their personal evolution, they want access to a team of well-informed, individually sensitive health professionals who can treat mind, body, and soul. They want a team of domestic professionals who can help them jettison mundane tasks in the maintenance of their residence and assets. They want a team of travel professionals who can organise risk-free journeys of discovery—across the city or across the globe. They want a team of cultural professionals who can help them choose challenging experiences and mind-full activities. And they want all of these services throughout their lives. Nothing is going to change just because they're getting older.

The physical form of the Peak Village will vary in scale, but it will have key, immutable characteristics. It will be architect-designed, with an emphasis on the beauty as well as the functionality of design. The overall setting will be created by a landscape architect to deliver equally to each resident the spirituality and harmony of a beautifully designed garden environment. Sustainability will be a core practice, with each residence having a five-star energy rating for the building fabric (the walls, ceilings, floors, and windows), and extensive water-saving initiatives, a rain-water tank, and a solar hot-water system as a bare minimum. An organic kitchen garden, chicken run, and organic orchard will provide fresh, clean produce and will give interested residents the opportunity to participate in the gardening process. Each residence will be completely independent, with privacy a key requirement.

While each residence will have a rudimentary but fully operational kitchen and laundry, a commercial kitchen and laundry will be sited centrally so that tasks considered temporarily or permanently mundane can be jettisoned to contracted visiting specialists. Special meals can be prepared by an imaginative contract chef, to be consumed either in individual residences or in the great room situated above the extensive wine cellar and adjacent to the library stocked with thousands of books, a large-screen home-entertainment system, DVDs, iPod speaker systems, a wireless modem for computers, and wireless routers connected to colour printers. Contracted specialists will deliver everything: medical services in the small but well-equipped clinic; shopping services, transport, gardening, dry cleaning, and maintenance; yoga classes in the library; massages in private residences; and computer services and pet care.

NEOs demand beauty, a seamlessly connected world, balance and tranquillity, intellectual stimulation, wonderful taste sensations, sustainability, and no compromises. They didn't compromise when they were forty, and they're not going to compromise at eighty. Sixty is the new No-Age. And so is eighty.

Many will stay in their own homes as their lives evolve; after all, less than 10 per cent of Australians over the age of 70 ever enter residential aged-care facilities. Others, however, will choose a Peak Village. Life for a NEO is all about choice.

Another service that NEOs will want to source is that of an advocate and a guide for navigating the issues of ageing and the inevitable bureaucratic complexity of dealing with government services and obligations such as tax, health care, and local government services.

NEOs in future will be looking for service-providers who are capable of creating and delivering peak experiences rather than a simulation of Traditional suburban life. The provision of such services in a NEO format will unlock latent demand and provide a sound foundation for a developer–consumer partnership as the population ages.

Even though spending traditionally decreases per capita after the age of 50, the volume of people over this age means that the 50-plus age bracket still collectively spends 60 per cent more than adults under 45. And with NEOs becoming an increasing proportion of the population aged over 50 in Australia in the next decade, their discretionary spending and propensity to 'invest' in quality experiences will shift with them, making this the new marketplace. But how many service-providers are ready for, or even aware of, the opportunities in this new marketplace?

There are, of course, physical changes that take place as we age, but many of them have already begun to impact our lives prior to retirement. Loss of visual acuity often begins early, but is most noticeable by the early forties. There are as many teenagers with some permanent hearing loss as there are people in the 45–65 age bracket (about 15 per cent). Taste and smell sensations also decline in acuity as we age, and have an impact on our relationship with the food that we eat. Our touch receptors decline, so that we are less tolerant of extremes in temperature and less able to detect changes in depth and texture. However, all these physical changes demand better design, not age-related design. And NEOs value design solutions throughout their lives.

The most important physical change to result directly from ageing is the progressive migration of mental activity from the analytical left-brain to the emotional right-brain mentioned earlier. It is important because it underlines how No-Age is the best age for NEOs. This physical process in our brains leads to a stronger sense of timelessness that results from having the range of peak experiences that younger NEOs dream about. It also makes us more sensitive to the metaphysical and symbolic—the very things that stimulate NEO consumption arousal.

The No-Age era means NEOs will behave as they wish, demanding good design, intelligent service provision, and peak experiences with no regard for whatever stage of life they may have reached.

No-Age is the best age.

18

God is Back, but No One's Kneeling

We hear much about the resurgence of religion around the world, in what is described by some as the post-secular age: the era in which secularism has failed, and resurgent religion is rushing to fill the void left by that failure. Many argue that as society becomes more materialistic the need for spirituality deepens, and would have us believe that we are all searching for:

> New sources of identity, new forms of stable community, and new sets of moral precepts to provide [us] with a sense of meaning and purpose ... there is a quest for some higher explanations about man's purpose, about why we are here. (*The Clash of Civilizations*, p. 97)

Religion has proven to be a decisive factor in recent presidential elections in the United States, and Islamic fundamentalism is never far from the nightly television news services. And while we see pockets of religious activism in Australia, notably the emergence of the Family First political party and the publicity-rich Hillsong church run by the photogenic Brian and Bobbie Houston, there is no discernable increase in religious activity across the country. Over the five

years since 2001, the number of Australians classifying themselves as religious has lifted by only 1 per cent from 72 to 73
per cent—hardly the end of the secular age and the resurgence of religious fervour to fill the vacuum. That's not to say
that religion is not important to many people; it is. However,
any hyperbole about its growth must be viewed within an evi-
dence-based context.

Undeniably, the media coverage of politicians visiting the
Houstons at Hillsong, the widening debate in the US about
the ironically named 'intelligent design' or creationism, and
the increasing invocation of God in politics around the world
demonstrates that God never really left the building—he is
back on the well-lit centre stage of noisy minorities.

Yet, despite the undiminished nature of our secular society,
in which mammon rather than God is dominant, we are
undoubtedly experiencing a yearning for deeper insights
and higher levels of spirituality. And while this yearning or
appetite is not being reflected in the growth of religious
observance in any traditional sense, it can be found in non-
traditional forms of spirituality and philosophy.

Traditional religion is less popular with NEOs than it is
with the rest of the population. By contrast, the self-reflection
and inner-directedness of yoga is, for example, very attractive: NEOs are twice as likely as Traditionals to participate in
yoga, because it offers myriad layers of physical, spiritual, and
exploratory challenge to an individual, is connected to a
global community, and is rich with the provenance of thousands of years of philosophy. The options of Yoga are endless,
but the discipline is exacting. It offers a perfect NEO pathway
to greater personal insight.

While NEO spirituality is as diverse and varied in practice
as would be expected of a group that represents 24 per cent
of the population, the hallmarks of NEO participation in

religious and spiritual practice are remarkably consistent. NEOs are attracted to beliefs, practices, and communities that offer doctrines with contemporary and personal relevance; that can stand the test of time; that offer personal growth, independent thinking, and an intelligent debate; whose provenance is deep and universally respected; whose practice is inclusive, active, and engaged with contemporary society and issues; and whose leadership is ethical and accountable. It's likely that NEOs will be more attracted to a particular religious or spiritual community through local, like-minded connections than through any overarching philosophical standpoint or a smart PR campaign.

NEOs are also fuelling a rising interest in spirituality in the business world through their involvement with socially responsible investing, shareholder activism, and demands for accountability in corporate governance. Because NEOs blur the lines between life, work, and play, the impact of their out-spoken voices and spending decisions will be felt more strongly than the behaviour of Traditionals, who are more likely to conform to the status quo. Because NEOs dominate business decision-making (72 per cent of all business pur-chase-decisions valued at more than $5000 are made or directly influenced by NEOs), their personal requirement for ethical, authentic, and well-informed decisions will also impact the business cultures they work in and buy from.

NEOs are sensitive to the so-called ripple effect on employees, suppliers, and shareholders of an unfair, unethical, or poorly justified business decision; a decision made without due consideration of the social consequences. The days of the decision-deities in corporate and political life are coming to an end. These are the God-like leaders who view employees and community resources as commodities to be moved and disposed of at will on the simulated game-board of their corporate universe. New accountability to deliver not only shareholder value but also a return on cultural capital will ensure that, while these God figures are omnipresent, no one's kneeling.

NEOs are ensuring that the game plan of decision-deities has radical new rules. NEOs were the early investors in ethical funds, are increasingly taking roles on boards, are at the forefront of shareholder activism, are influencing the regulators and opinion leaders in the media, and understand better than anyone else how important it is for an organisation to demonstrate sustainability by delivering increasing returns on cultural capital, and on social responsibility.

However, while God has re-emerged in politics, and the practical manifestations of a more spiritual society are surfacing in boardrooms, we aren't going to church any more than we were five years ago, and less than we were a decade before. Rather than religion filling the void of a post-secular world, temporal spirituality is instead filling the vacuum left by the failure of traditional religion to make any real headway over the past twenty years.

For NEOs, this new temporal spirituality needs to be active. The idea that their fate is already decided, and that nothing can be done to change their fortune, is not for them. Their high locus of control makes them unable to sit on the sidelines and observe. Their connection to the world through the Internet makes them better informed and more vocal; however, it doesn't make them any more likely to have identified a higher purpose or to have found a grand unified theory of being. Politically active and socially progressive organisations such as GetUp.org.au offer NEOs a fast and efficient way to influence and participate in the emergence of a world characterised by social equity and progressive values. Many NEOs are actively participating in yoga; others are mounting the ethical barricades to change the behaviour of political and corporate organizations; and others are embarking on journeys of self-discovery that look more like five-star experiences in the Daintree than the dirty days of Nimbin.

The future of spirituality and religion looks strong, but it doesn't look much like religion of the past.

God is back, but no one's kneeling.

19

Fascinomas are Redefining Desire

Fascinoma (*Noun*: medical slang for a fascinating case, usually involving a rare disease)

In a world where the act of spending money accompanies most of our daily activities, either as a requirement or a consequence, desire has become inextricably linked with consumption. NEOs are redefining desire, frequently giving consumption a higher discretionary character than ever before. It's not the act of consumption that is given extra weight, but the process of discretionary consumption—the research, selection, enjoyment, and retelling of it. It really doesn't matter how much is spent, but rather how it is spent. NEOs care about the money they earn only because it fuels their ability to express who they are and who they might be tomorrow. For NEOs, consumption is fuelled by desire.

In all populations there is a wide range of behaviours and expressions. If we look at NEOs as a population of four million, we have enough information to detect meaningful differences in their behaviours. For example, having accepted the evidence that NEOs spend more than anyone else in society, we can take a look at the difference between the top and bottom deciles of NEO spending. And we find that the top 10 per cent behave quite differently to the bottom 10 per cent. Those in the top decile spend more intensely (in fewer categories) and more deeply (more money per category). There is more refinement in their spending and it is more idiosyncratic. This is to be expected in a global economy where NEOs can find exactly what they want, when they want it. But since this expenditure is being driven by a set of deeply personal motivations and interests, it finds itself on the outer limits of the discretionary-spending orbit.

Let's imagine a 'discretionary wheel' with basic-needs consumption—that is, the necessities of life—at its centre or hub. The wheel is an apt metaphor because it has remained constant throughout history and no one can reinvent it. And, like most powerful concepts, our 'discretionary wheel' doesn't have a hard boundary. Rather, it has a gravitational core—the further you move away from the core, the stronger the gravitational pull.

Around that central hub is a circle of low-discretionary consumption that might include bottled water rather than tap water, an organic chicken-and-avocado sandwich rather than a cheese-and-tomato roll, or a barista-made long-black espresso rather than an instant coffee. Outside that circle is another ring of discretionary consumption, spending on self-expression, that might cover our social and intellectual needs: this might include following an 'art trail' of museums and galleries in Europe, staying at W Hotels, and flying business class with Qantas; or having an architect design the living-room extension; or adding to a small collection of Movado watches; or buying a second fountain pen in the Marc Chagall series by Marlen.

After traversing a number of widening and increasingly rarefied circles, we arrive at the outside ring: the orbit of deep desire, of extreme discretionary consumption where the symbolic and imaginative nature of the rare experience reigns supreme. We call this idiosyncratic, narrowly focussed, ultra-refined fascination with rare experiences a Fascinoma.

The question is often posed in a society in which luxury has become more commonplace, 'What comes next? What is beyond the new luxury that seems to touch every aspect of our lives?' The answer is Fascinoma.

While a Fascinoma has no purpose in the traditional sense, it does have the unintended consequence of creating new perspectives and sometimes new trends in the wider world. This takes it beyond the hobby, beyond a passion for objects, beyond the generalised pursuit of a powerful interest, to a place at the extreme limits of consumption; a place so powerful that its whisper is heard, like the flap of the butterfly's wing, across the globe.

Consider Maslow's famous hierarchy of needs with the peak experience at the top of the pyramid: this is where we find the Fascinoma.

Most people never experience a Fascinoma, and are delighted with activities that are much more tangible and, to them, no less rewarding. Imagine for example, someone whose hobby is collecting. Typically, this will be a Traditional collecting readymade objects that are valued for themselves as individual items and for the aggregated completeness of the collection. That is well below the peak experience. It is important to the collector, certainly, and to the community of collectors in which he moves, but it is not a Fascinoma.

Trucking magnate Lindsay Fox's car collection and Mambo director Wayne Golding's snowdome collection may both be the largest in Australia, and they no doubt result from a driving passion in each case, but they are simply wonderful collections of things made by someone else that cannot be changed or influenced regardless of who collects them. In those two cases, neither collector exerts any real influence on the car or snowdome industry, or on their aesthetics.

Nor does the Japanese woman who has collected 715 of the 750 limited-edition versions of the Fendi bagette since it came onto the market. Fendi has not (yet) designed a bag to honour this woman, and so she appears to have little influence on Fendi or other handbag designers. She is simply a collector—though certainly at a high-level of discretionary consumption.

A Fascinoma is a rare and uniquely personal expedition masquerading as consumption. Take, for example, Charles Saatchi, the famous founder of global advertising giant Saatchi & Saatchi and, subsequently, M&C Saatchi. Saatchi made his fortune during a stellar and often controversial career in advertising. It is not, however, his occupation that is relevant. In the early 1970s Charles Saatchi bought a painting during a visit to Paris, and this proved to be the first step on what was to become one of the greatest-ever expeditions into the world of contemporary art. Saatchi started off as a collector; but his fascination, bordering on obsession, became so overwhelming that he became an art patron to rival the Medici. However, this was no safe journey of acquisition.

Saatchi acquired young, radical, often controversial, artists and transformed their status from oblivion to fame almost overnight. He makes numerous visits in person to exhibitions, as well as seeking out artists' studios and little-known back-street galleries, particularly in East London, in order to discover innovative work. Saatchi developed the golden touch, and by 1997 his renown was at a peak when part of his collection was shown at the Royal Academy as the exhibition 'Sensation'. The exhibition also travelled to museums in Berlin and New York, causing headlines and controversy, and consolidated the prime position of the group known as the Young British Artists, or YBAs, whom he had made famous. The Saatchi collection is reportedly worth as much as $500 million.

Advertising was Charles Saatchi's occupation. An expedition into the uncharted sea of undiscovered contemporary art was his Fascinoma.

The recent growth in multiplayer online role-playing games (known as MMOs) gives us a picture of another ingredient of the Fascinoma—imagination. And how quickly Fascinomas can develop where the constraints of geographical distance and real time are collapsed. *Second Life* is a type of game which doesn't have a specific narrative (or goal-oriented structure) and which gives 'émigrés' a tool kit to build and create whatever they want in a much faster time-frame than in the real world. In an article by Roger Parloff in *Fortune* magazine (28 November 2005), a German schoolteacher describes how she (actually, her avatar, or virtual self) worked through several careers in this virtual world that enabled her to buy virtual land and rent it out or resell it. Other people in the virtual world earn money by being rental managers or developers of entertainment venues. As MMOs have developed, the internal currency has become monetised in the real world, as new players join and the demand for virtual resources increases. The German schoolteacher's entirely idiosyncratic participation is influencing a whole world of consumption. And virtual money, converted into real money, is providing the currency of fascination.

Her job was teaching in a German school. Her Fascinoma was leading a lucrative, imaginative second life in a world that is as real to her as the world of parents and pupils.

Because NEOs so often blur the lines between life, work, and play, Fascinomas are already more prevalent in the world of work. In another demonstration of the underlying reason why NEOs earn above-average salaries, they earn more because their underlying attitudes and values lead them to embark on an expedition of discovery and challenge rather than the tried-and-true ladder to the boss's job. They are more likely to ask for a pay rise, more likely to change jobs to pursue a more stimulating work life or a new line of work altogether. They are more likely to develop a deep knowledge of a topic area quickly, and then use that knowledge to move into a new area. Wherever imagination and influence are given rein, a NEO will follow the deep veins of desire and curiosity—whether it is in work or play. So working in a particular content area will drive NEO desire and curiosity, which in turn drives demand for consumption in that content area (books, magazines, seminars, online subscriptions, tools, and outfits). In a virtuous spiral, NEOs bring demand with them wherever they work. And as the idea of work becomes more open and less reliant on an existing business or organisational format, NEOs will allow their desire to fuel their work choices.

Imagine starting a career in a law firm, specialising in intellectual property, and then discovering the field of virtual property rights—the kind that are required when real-money trade takes place inside a virtual game world. Needing to understand the game you begin to play it, and you discover that there is demand inside this world for intellectual-property lawyers to advise the real-world people whose avatars have created wealth and virtual property. But you can also take your legal avatar and create a new kind of legal service that is not possible in the bricks-and-mortar world. You can take your curiosity and your desire, and have them play out in the virtual world, creating a new perspective in the virtual world but also changing the way you view your bricks-and-mortar legal job. There are legal seminars to attend around the world, and games gatherings, too. So is it leisure or is it work?

It's easy to see how a Fascinoma can begin. Desire mixes with imagination, and yearning intersects with opportunity. Expeditions take place to the outside ring, the orbit of deep desire, of extreme discretionary consumption where the symbolic and imaginative nature of the rare experience reigns supreme. This is where we find the Fascinoma.

Fascinomas are redefining desire.

-20-
Water is the New Oil

This book focuses on discretionary spending, the definition of which is 'spending that goes beyond satisfying basic needs and is subject to individual judgment or discretion'.

In our day jobs, we frequently ask interested individuals to nominate which retail brand they think best represents spending on basic needs, and which brand stands for discretionary spending. Typically, Woolworths and David Jones are nominated on each side of the discretionary divide. Our interviewees are then asked to identify the ultimate discretionary consumer product sold, paradoxically, in the basic-needs supermarket. The usual answer is 'chocolate'; sometimes, and less glamorously, it is 'toilet paper'. Perhaps the most profound answer, however, is 'bottled water'.

To understand just how extraordinary this is, transport yourself back only 20 years, and imagine a slick salesman trying to convince you that one of the world's most common commodities is set to become one of its most valuable. How incredulous you would be to hear that water — the ubiquitous liquid that falls free from the sky, to be gathered easily and consumed by anyone — would be sold in plastic bottles in supermarkets and specialty stores, and that it would be bought in such volumes that the Coca-Cola Company would sell pure, filtered bottled water alongside its traditional iconic product.

In fact, in modern-day Australia almost 600 million litres of water a year are packaged and sold under more than 1,000 water brands to thirsty Australians by beverage giants such as Coca-Cola Amatil and Schweppes, and by boutique companies, both local and international. Even wine and beer giant Foster's has expanded into bottled water.

However, is this new obsession with water limited to the discretionary purchase in the supermarket? Is it symptomatic of a world increasingly fascinated by talk of well-being and healthy lifestyles? Or is it a portent of other, larger, perhaps more sinister trends?

There is, undoubtedly, a shift to concern for wellbeing and an associated thirst for purity, the organic, and the unprocessed. This shift has been accelerated by very clever brand marketing and the creation of a fierce new fashion for the water bottle constantly at one's side or at one's lips, perhaps recalling in adults a longing for the comfort of the baby's bottle. There is, however, a parallel phenomenon occurring that makes this new fashionable use of water deeply paradoxical.

Global warming, or what is known more politely as climate change, is being blamed for the global reduction in available potable water. Never before have we been more aware of the need to capture, save, recycle, redistribute, reprocess, and value common water. Scenarios are being run in which participants project a world without discretionary potable water, of a time when water has indeed become one of the most valuable elements on earth. Immediately the futurists introduce privatisation and invoke a sense of deep commercial value, the dynamic changes to one inescapable conclusion: water is to the 21st century what oil was to the 20th century.

In Britain, the London authorities have introduced the

most pernicious water restrictions in that city's long history. In India, many of the world's most populous urban centres are facing a water crisis. Even for India's 300 million well-heeled urban middle class, water is typically available for only two hours a day. Public water stands and taps are locked to the citizens for most of the day, and local authorities are battling to prevent corrupt tanker drivers and public officials selling tanks of water to corporations that bottle and sell it at a huge profit. And in the middle of this Indian water crisis is Delhi, the host city for the 2010 Commonwealth Games. How it deals with the huge influx of visitors placing Delhi firmly in the global gaze remains to be seen, but its agenda includes a heated debate about the privatisation of water. Indian academic and social commentator Dr. Vandana Shiva believes 'Delhi needs to learn from the privatisation tragedies of Manila, Buenos Aires, South Africa where privatisation has meant unsafe water at high prices for the consumers, and higher debts and financial burdens for impoverished public systems.'

In Australia, permanent water restrictions are in place for most capitals; while this seems explicable for parched Adelaide, it is unthinkable for sub-tropical Brisbane, which is experiencing its worst drought in 100 years.

Against this backdrop, businesses are sucking hundreds of millions of litres of potable water each year out of Australia's subterranean lakes or aquifers for the bottled-water market. The dramatically reduced rainfall is insufficient to replenish the aquifers, while industry and agriculture continue to either divert or consume huge volumes of water with unabated thirst.

Conclusion? The scarcity of water and the rapidly widening impact of global warming are important future drivers of economic and social change. Water is the first global victim of the climate change we have wrought upon ourselves. The shift of a product from an everyday to a luxury item occurs most dramatically when demand intersects with scarcity. NEOs will be the forerunners of consumption trends that re-value water and, by elevating its status beyond that of a commodity, move it from secondary into tertiary consumption.

Melbourne designer Katrina Logan has 'tapped into' this trend by producing a rainwater tank for urban backyards that is as beautiful as it is functional. Covered in a rich-coloured satin acrylic case that makes a design statement by day, it is lit internally by LEDs to create a different effect at night. Katrina's commitment is to create awareness, not by nagging and preaching but by creating a tank that offers an alternative to the 'blokey plumber's' style of products designed for a rural market. She wanted to make rain tanks 'sexy', and who better than NEOs to design for? The casing is, 'like a sheath, a beautiful piece of clothing over an ordinary tank, that creates a mysterious effect, like looking at a body through a frosted window or shower screen'. Containers must now become vessels that are worthy of the precious fluid that falls from the sky. And, as we have seen, NEOs will always choose function mediated by design and beauty ahead of pure function alone.

The acquisition by water of a new symbolic value will cause NEOs to find ways to embrace and celebrate it. In the same way that NEOs understand the different value of commercial chicken at $7/kg, organic chicken at $12/kg and Saskia Beer's Barossa chicken at $32/kg, they'll begin to use the same distinctions with water. *Gourmet Traveller* magazine will specify rainwater in its recipes at first, and then move to featuring brand-name waters that can be guaranteed earth-friendly and pure. Expect water purity and scarcity to be emphasised in spa treatments, cosmetics, and other personal grooming rituals. Expect new domestic rainwater harvesting with purity monitoring. Expect new travel experiences that celebrate fresh, clear, pure water, which may even begin to challenge the symbolic value of the beach and sea water in our culture. A pristine mountain lake or stream will be as attractive a destination as a coral reef.

In Majorca, travellers may visit Tristan, a waterfront restaurant that boasts, in addition to an extensive wine list, an equally extensive water list featuring ten sparkling and 15 still waters, with a detailed description of each. Prices range up to 16 Euros ($27) for a small bottle; and in sunny Spain, many small bottles are required for just one meal.

Water has a deep historical, religious, and cultural provenance for NEOs to explore and engage with. Expect to see water-based concepts and images incorporated into leading-edge design, luxury fashion, and architecture as NEOs translate their exploration of water and its new symbolic value into consumption goods.

Water is the new oil.

Private is the New Public

It seems paradoxical, or perhaps logical, that we are becoming more private as the world becomes more public, as reality television makes human behaviour more public, and as communication barriers disappear, making it possible to be reached anywhere on the globe.

In a world that is increasingly institutionalised, we are becoming more individual; in a world with countless choices, we are designing our own options; in a world that corporatises everything, we are becoming more personal. This is the NEO credo.

One explanation for this trend is that people are evolving and changing faster than the organisations that employ them and sell to them. Shoshana Zuboff, Professor of Business Administration at Harvard Business School, believes that an important indicator of how much people have changed in the last 50 years is to be found in higher-education trends. If you take US data on higher-education enrolment, he says, and give it an index value of 100 in 1955, it had achieved a value of 600 by the year 2000. He then suggests taking a key business indicator such as return on assets (ROA), again giving it an index value of 100 in 1955. In this case, ROA had declined to a score of 3 by the year 2000. Even allowing for dramatically changed economic conditions over the period of the study, the return on assets has failed to match the spectacular rise in higher-education enrolments. The individual thirst for knowledge is growing at a faster rate than institutional success.

However, education is only one of the indications that people are evolving faster than institutions. After all, the Internet is the epitome of a decorporatised universe where individuals rather than institutions rule, and the shift from corporate websites to personal blogs serves to confirm this reversal. And blog-dominating NEOs are at the forefront of privatising a corporatised society.

This trend can also be seen in entertainment and the arts. Just as concert halls and performance arenas become bigger and bigger, some forms of entertainment are becoming minuscule and intensely private. In 2005, for example, Polish Teatr Rozmaitosci, located in Warsaw, started performing their play *Mleko* (*Milk*) in living rooms and kitchens of private homes, providing individuals with their own performance during lunch times or evenings. The cost of a private living-room play was $250. In Melbourne, the iconic Australian Centre for Contemporary Art, or ACCA, offers visitors the opportunity to download onto their own iPod a personal podguide in advance of a visit to a new exhibition, ensuring that their private visit to a public space is rich and singular.

Never before have we had more opportunities to privatise our experiences. For example, there was a time when, to buy a house, we had to cram into an uncomfortable real estate office and make public our interest as we looked through flyers and brochures, asked questions in public, and clutched in our hands the real estate ads from that morning's news-paper. Today, we simply turn on the computer in the morning and instantly receive relevant and personalised information on potential houses in direct response to the filters we entered in the privacy of our own homes. Every aspect of the public world can be more private if we wish to make it so.

The most popular and financially successful 'product' offered by Yahoo! is the online service known as 'personals'. This is the dating or matchmaking service that has revolutionised 'boy meets girl' or 'girl meets girl' or any other permutation of gender mix. Once, a smart 30-something girl with a degree, an interesting job, and a great sense of humour would have to suffer the indignity and potential public humiliation of standing around in a bar or other public space to meet an interesting guy. When she did, the chances were that she was initially attracted to him because he was the right height and, more importantly, liked the same wine she did. Alas, a long hour later, she would discover to her horror that the only thing they had in common was the wine.

Now, in the privacy of her own home, she can assess potential dates by checking their interests, activities, and expectations online. She can create a shortlist of men who have similar personal interests and professional ambitions, and talk to them privately on the phone before agreeing to meet one or two for lunch or a drink. Certainly, the process doesn't allow for emotional chemistry or physical or mental attraction; but it does reduce the risk of time-wasting and it does make the process of finding a mate much more private than the public alternative.

The emergence of private, and more personal, service-providers in direct competition to their publicly listed cousins can also be witnessed in the financial-services sector. Zopa, a private online 'lending and borrowing exchange', connects people who want to borrow money with people who want to lend it. The lenders are private individuals who set their own interest rates and select the people to whom they will lend their money.

The Zopa value proposition is straightforward and three-fold: 'Our Borrowers are Better Than Banks'; 'Our Lenders are Better Than Banks'; and 'People are Better Than Banks.'

Zopa says it's obvious that people are better than banks. They're better at playing football; better at going out for dinner with; better at painting watercolours; better because they don't have shareholders. 'We don't have sales targets,' they say, 'and we definitely don't have a one-size-fits-all mentality.'

At Zopa, they also declare their love for podcasts, 'because they annoy the establishment who don't get the potential; because they were invented by users of one technology putting it to a new purpose; because anyone can post one and become an instant broadcaster.' This doesn't sound like any public or institutional bank we know.

Reportedly, Zopa has 26,000 members, 35 per cent of whom are lenders, and most loans are for between $5,000 and $10,000, with the average rate of return for the lenders at 7.6 per cent. Zopa makes money by charging lenders and borrowers a fee—borrowers pay 0.5 per cent of their loan amount, and lenders pay a 0.5 per cent annual service fee.

Communicating around the globe has become increasingly commonplace and, until recently, increasingly expensive. A conference call on a public telephone network with a caller in Sydney, one in Melbourne and two in different locations in London can cost hundreds of dollars. Many are therefore moving from the public phone system to a new way of communicating. Voice over Internet Protocol or VoIP was, until recently, a fringe activity embraced passionately by tech-heads and *very* early adopters. However, with the advent of Skype and other VoIP providers, the world has changed.

Skype, as one example of a VoIP provider, enables users

to download simple software in a few minutes and then to make a call using a $60 headset plugged into the computer to a colleague or friend anywhere in the world. If the friend also has Skype loaded and a headset, they can talk for free for hours—or days, if they have the stamina. If the friend doesn't have Skype loaded or isn't near their computer, a call can be made to any fixed line or mobile number for one or two dollars an hour.

The experience of telephony has changed irrevocably, and has gone from a public process to a very private one.

Corporations are deciding whether to stay private or to go private. Service-providers are making the process more private. Borrowing money is more private, and even finding a boyfriend has become more private.

Private is the new public.

-22-

How Many Light Globes Does it Take to Change a Culture?

Once, the gatekeepers in our society made and enforced the rules. Bank managers decided if we were fortunate enough to get a home loan, doctors decided how we should be treated, programmers decided what we should see on television or at the movies, and content managers determined what we would find in the information silos known as websites. Now, however, the gates are opening and the gatekeepers are out of a job.

A columnist for the *New Yorker* magazine, James Surowiecki, recently published *Wisdom of Crowds*, a book that explores a deceptively simple idea that has profound implications: large groups of people are smarter than an elite few, no matter how brilliant they might be—better at solving problems, fostering innovation, coming to wise decisions, even predicting the future.

In his book, Surowiecki uses the example of the hit television show *Who Wants to be a Millionaire?* He argues that, every week, *Millionaire* pitted group intelligence against individual intelligence—and that, every week, group intelligence won:

Who Wants to Be a Millionaire? was a simple show in terms of structure: a contestant was asked multiple-choice questions, which got successively more difficult, and if she answered fifteen questions in a row correctly, she walked away with $1 million. The show's gimmick was that if a contestant got stumped by a question, she could pursue three avenues of assistance. First, she could have two of the four multiple-choice answers removed (so she'd have at least a fifty-fifty shot at the right response). Second, she could place a call to a friend or relative, a person whom, before the show, she had singled out as one of the smartest people she knew, and ask him or her for the answer. And third, she could poll the studio audience, which would immediately cast its votes by computer. Everything we think we know about intelligence suggests that the smart individual would offer the most help. And, in fact, the 'experts' did okay, offering the right answer—under pressure—almost 65 percent of the time. But they paled in comparison to the audiences. Those random crowds of people with nothing better to do on a weekday afternoon than sit in a TV studio picked the right answer 91 percent of the time.

Collective intelligence is more powerful than the intelligence of an individual. Creative directors for major events are increasingly floating ideas on talk-back radio stations that have high NEO audiences—frequently, ABC Radio's talk shows—and, no matter how brilliant their concepts were at the outset, after twenty minutes of talk-back calls they walk away with a swagful of new and wonderful ideas.

The light globe of a bright idea switching-on above someone's head is a friendly and familiar image. This trend of crowd intelligence makes the familiar light-globe imagery even more apposite when we realise that the light from a million globes is more illuminating than that from just a few.

Websites are being increasingly curated not by content managers, but by users. Imagine NEOplanet, a virtual space where NEOs go to find information about NEO experiences around the world. A user taps in 'breakfast in New York', and within a nanosecond a web-crawler, pre-programmed with NEO filters, has identified 20 options for a delicious NEO breakfast in Manhattan. However, that's not the whole story; in fact, it's not the story at all. Within seconds, NEOs across the globe are reviewing the web-crawler's choices and providing online suggestions about the excellent boiled egg and toast 'soldiers' at Balthazar in Spring Street, SoHo; and, more importantly, NEOs are whispering to the enquirer, and a million other users, about their own secret discoveries they have made in search of the perfect breakfast in New York. If a Traditional stumbles onto the site and recommends an all-you-can-eat breakfast for only $10 with fantastic hash browns and corn-beef hash that fills the plate and fills your stomach, NEOs will edit-out within minutes the non-NEO suggestion. Control is not in the hands of a few experts; ask a question, and light globes go on around the world.

This model is already well established and is sometimes referred to as a wiki, a curious term that Simon van Wyk, head of HotHouse Interactive in Sydney, describes as a shortened version of the Hawaiian phrase 'wiki wiki', meaning quick or fast. Van Wyk describes a wiki as, 'undoubtedly the fastest, most community-oriented way to build content and information about a subject'.

The world's largest and most influential wiki is *Wikipedia*, an online encyclopaedia that is written and maintained by volunteers and users. *Wikipedia* is now, says van Wyk, used by more people than *Encyclopaedia Britannica* or any other reference website. 'Honesty and accuracy are sometimes an issue, but Wikipedia claims that incorrect entries are corrected or removed within five minutes of posting.'

Created in 2001, *Wikipedia* offers more than 1.2 million articles in English, compared with *Encyclopaedia Britannica*'s

80,000, and *Encarta*'s 4500, written by more than 16,000 contributors. It is the exemplar for users storming the gates of the fortress.

Even that doyen of traditional media, Rupert Murdoch, seems to be getting the message. He told the American Society of Newspaper Editors that too many editors and reporters are out of touch with their readers. He said that today's teens, 20-somethings, and 30-somethings 'don't want to rely on a so-called life figure from above to tell them what's important. As an industry, many of us have been remarkably, unaccountably, complacent'.

The shift from gate-keeper to user is also found in pockets of the online retail sector. For example, following the popularity of US-based Threadless, the continuing t-shirt design competition that urges users to submit t-shirt designs, a European version has been spawned. Like Threadless, the newly formed Derby is a design competition. People are invited to send in designs which, over a period of ten days, are scored by Derby's visitors. The designs with the highest scores are printed on high-quality t-shirts and sold through the site's shop, and the winner gets almost $1,000.

Similar initiatives exist in France (La Fraise), Germany (Cyroline), and the Netherlands (Buutvrij), but Derby is the first pan-European player, and was launched in English, German, and French. Besides selling winning t-shirts online, Derby has also opened a real-world shop on Gabelsberger Street in Berlin.

Derby was created by Spreadshirt, a large German print-on-demand company that lets users design and print their own t-shirts and other merchandise, and sell them on their own Spreadshirt pages.

While previously the style mavens would whisper to NEOs what the 'hot' look was for the upcoming season, now NEOs have the confidence or curiosity to become their own style maven.

Frustrated that a favourite colour of lipstick or tie—the one you love because of how it makes you feel and what it says to you about who you have become—is no longer available? Then get it custom-made. A US company called 3C will take your favourite colour and create lip colour, blush, or eye shadow exclusively for you, and then store your 'recipe' in its permanent files for easy re-ordering.

In Australia, readers are having more influence than ever before on newspapers. The editors of traditional newspapers are increasingly looking to their online partners for inspiration, and are finding that blogs offer a rich source, not only of feedback, but also of new and innovative content. This trend will continue in the future, with as much as one-third of the editorial content of a newspaper coming from readers who are not on the payroll. This is a good example of the much-vaunted communications–media convergence coming to fruition, albeit very differently from the original idea that the media and media operators would converge. No one imagined that it would be the content, the ideas, and the imaginations of millions of individuals that would so revolutionise the media and the Internet. After all ...

How many light globes does it take to change a culture?

23

Design is the New Passion

How do NEOs come to understand themselves and their place in the world? In the next decade, one way will be through design—graphic design, interior design, garden design, architecture, and industrial design. From mobile phones to motorways, t-shirts to office towers, graphics to typography, design has an impact on how we understand and experience the world.

Design directly touches the human mind and the human spirit. It springs from a passion for more beauty in an increasingly ugly world, and so it is that design has assumed a dominant place in the hearts and minds of aesthetic NEOs.

In the trend of design exemplifying desire, Apple's iPod has become the new I Ching. This ancient Chinese philosophy encompassed 'the dynamic balance of opposites, the evolution of events, and an acceptance of the inevitability of change'. What better description could there be for the piece of design that is an archetype of the revolution of the music industry and a symbol of its intersection with consumer electronics and the Information Age? The iPod is a product that is beyond product definition. It is the very avatar of the inevitability of change.

Functional products that are also beautiful give our lives

meaning and purpose. Virginia Postrel, in her book *The Substance of Style*, describes this change as 'design moving from the abstract and ideological — "this is good design" — to the personal and the emotional — "I *like* that."'

NEOs are less passionate about possessions — that is more typically the territory of Traditionals. NEOs desire experiences which recognise that there is life beyond functionality: that experiences matter more than things, that ideas and concepts can be captured without words, that not everything that has value can be owned and produced by a corporation. NEOs have moved on — they are deeply engaged with experiences and meanings. How things look and feel are just as important as what they do.

The first step for information-hungry NEOs is usually to tap into the wellsprings of knowledge in a particular area by buying specialist books and also understanding its current incarnation in specialist magazines. NEOs are four times more likely to purchase quality design and lifestyle magazines than non-NEOs, and this growing interest of NEOs has fuelled a huge growth in this sector of the magazine industry. In 2000, five new titles were launched in this sector in Australia, and since then the total number has soared past twenty-five.

The impact of this change on how we live, work, and play will be profound. Currently, only around 3 per cent of the population choose an architect to design their new home — a small percentage of the overall housing market. But imagine the impact of an increase in demand for design and beauty. The current housing stock in Australia is valued at something approaching $2,000 billion; and each year, according to the Australian Bureau of Statistics, an additional $5 billion is spent on new housing. A rough calculation, therefore, shows that architects account for $150m of residential work each year, and that for every 1 per cent of additional residential work undertaken by architects, the impact on the economy will be another $50 million.

More and more, in specialised residential developments, all housing is being designed by architects; and in other market-led quality developments the proportion is as high as 75 per cent. This trend towards beauty and design in the residential market will ensure that, increasingly, in our places of rest and reflection we will find quietude and meditation; a sign of change that will transform the familiar idea of a suburb as a collection of homes of roughly similar functions and forms to a tangible, visible commitment to design, diversity, and individuality. All these are elements that satisfy deep desire in NEOs.

The impact on workspaces will also be profound, and is already visible. The new head office for the National Australia Bank (rebranded recently as 'nab') at Melbourne's Docklands was specifically designed with a culture change in mind, and is one of very few examples in Australia where a new office building has created anything other than a 21st-century version of a white-collar factory. NAB's office spaces serve the same banking management and administration functions as before, but they look and feel distinctly different and more beautiful; more designed.

It's not just the functions that are being re-designed in this new era of design beauty. The aesthetics of the personal experience are at last starting to be taken into consideration. The new Westpac head office in Sydney's CBD has taken the same set of functions that were performed in the old buildings and re-valued them. Now the 'work' experience of drinking coffee in a meeting has been elevated to being equivalent to the 'play' experience of drinking coffee: meet a Westpac team in one of their conference rooms, and a barista will serve you a restaurant-quality coffee, on restaurant-quality china, and topped off with a tiny crisp cookie, just as you would expect if you were meeting friends or colleagues in any other CBD café. NEOs in these offices breathe a sigh of relief, but wonder why it's taken so long to integrate such a basic part of daily culture into the organisation. Contrast this experience to having a meeting in the Coles Myer head office windowless workspaces in Melbourne's Tooronga, not-so-affectionately known as 'the bunker'. It is an entirely functional building, built in the 1980s and little-changed since. It is, however, entirely appropriate for a company whose customer-base is dominated by Traditionals.

Companies at the forefront of discretionary spending are beginning to realise that, as Postrel so neatly describes it, the consideration of aesthetics has become too important to be left to the aesthetes. The Starwood Group have been a forerunner in differentiating their hotels through design. They did this first with the 5-star W Hotel chain that sought out individually distinctive buildings to create a design that had individuality and diversity built in. Now they've taken on the motel experience with their ALOFT brand, planning to roll out 500 roadside and airport motels by 2012. They'll use natural materials and high-tech services to create a 'designed' experience at the lower end of the price spectrum, focussing on creating enticing public spaces that draw people out of their rooms.

'Luxury is not what something costs,' says the designer David Rockwell in *Surface* magazine. 'Luxury has more to do with a kind of sensibility and a sense of sophistication. Consumers appreciate smart design more than anything else, and they respond to things that make them feel good'. Well, at least that's true of NEOs who spend more and travel more.

No discussion of aesthetics and design would be complete without reference to the visual arts. Australian artist and academic Peter Hill says cultural tourism is here to stay. Events such as the Venice Biennale, the Basel Art Fair, the documenta, and the Munster Sculpture Project all attract high-spending NEOs as cultural tourists, and provide them with an art trail across central Europe.

The documenta occurs in the small German town of Kassel and, according to Hill, operates on a budget of more than $30 million and is regarded as the pre-eminent art event in the world. It is, he says, far more curatorially rigorous, for example, than the Venice Biennale, runs for several months, and attracts millions of visitors.

Beautiful art and beautiful design sometimes meet, as in the case of IM Pei's exquisite East Wing of the National Gallery of Art, Washington, D.C. Pei is perhaps more famous for his controversial pyramid structure at the Louvre in Paris. Another example of art meeting art is Frank Gehry's sculptural masterpiece in the small Spanish city of Bilbao. The design he created for the Guggenheim Bilbao delivers proof-positive that design can be harnessed to serve mammon without losing its integrity. In commercial terms, Gehry's architecture and the Guggenheim's art have proved such an irresistible combination that approximately one million people visit the Guggenheim Bilbao every year, only 17 per cent of whom are locals. This fascination with art and design yields more than $300 million to the local economy, representing the equivalent of almost 5000 jobs. That's not generated by a new manufacturing plant or huge software office park. That's all the work of an art museum.

Buildings like Guggenheim and events like documenta put cities on the global map, are economically robust, and are good for tourism and civic pride. As Peter Hill says of art events, they brand a city in relation to its neighbours. 'Get these things right and you create jobs, and people want to move to your city to fill those jobs and support your housing market.'

The design tsunami is also reaching our otherwise functional airlines. Important parts of the future flying experience, dominated as it is by NEOs, whether for business or leisure, are being curated for Qantas by leading designers, but are being driven by a clear business and marketing strategy to attract, engage, and retain valuable NEOs. In a forward-thinking move, Qantas has given responsibility to Recaro for the complete redesign of seats in their new economy-class cabins. Recaro is legendary for designing perfect precision seats for Formula 1 cars. Marc Newson, the iconoclastic Australian designer, has designed the new Qantas business-class beds, and has been instrumental in redefining the concept of an airline lounge from one of traditional comfort and function to one of beauty, design, and the treasured experience.

It is no longer enough to have a lounge with chairs, work desks, power points, and coffee machines. NEOs will assume that this kind of functionality is present and is the best an airline can do; it will merely be a hygiene factor in their spending decisions. Their deciding vote will be cast through an emotional connection with a positive and uplifting experience. Design will be the key that unlocks this vote because design can make connections at the symbolic and aesthetic level that is entirely and uniquely personal. And where else than in an international airport is feeling like a valued and understood individual more important?

The next stage for NEOs embracing design is through curated experiences that have design and a strong aesthetic at their heart. Traditionals may, for example, decide to eat at the Kitchen Table at Matt Moran's Aria Restaurant to boast that they have done it, but NEOs will desire to eat close to the action so that they can 'breathe' the same air and gain some insight into the chef's process and philosophy that can help their own food mastery. Sydney's Top 3 By Design leaves NEOs in no doubt as to what is 'hot' in the design world across a range of domestic and personal categories. NEOs love smart, independent lists that deliver a neat range of options to choose from. Expect to see more sales in this format in future. Even Third Drawer Down, by producing limited-edition, beautifully designed tea towels and aprons, understands that design matters to NEOs every day.

NEOs learn through their experiences, and as they gain confidence in their own knowledge they will select a few trusted information sources and an even smaller number of trusted suppliers who can reliably and consistently help them see the 'leading edge'. And then they want to get more involved, more hands-on. Crossing the experience divide on design has already begun, facilitated by savvy businesses that can see and animate a connection between NEOs and their products and services. In an exemplary demonstration of how to engage NEOs across their design-discovery experiences, the US design magazine *Surface* created a 'pop-up' (that is, short-term) gallery and retail space in New York to showcase interior design based on the Bombay Sapphire gin brand imagery. Bombay Sapphire has built its recent brand image around design, making the distinctive blue glass bottle the challenge and inspiration for design competitions.

Design inhabits every category of our lives. Every time we walk down a city street we are surrounded by design decisions: some are beautiful, some not. Our computers are designed, as are our iPods; our televisions; our knives and forks; our wine glasses; the label on our wine bottle; our cars;

our plane seats; our shoes; even, sadly, our pets. In the past, however, design has largely been of a functional and industrial nature, with only the fortunate few enjoying the beauty of an architect-designed interior living space.

Design is coming out of the back room and into the spotlight as NEOs, yearning for balance and beauty, are insisting on it in every aspect of their lives. More and more consumers can afford it, and even those who can't afford to invest in a new architect-designed home will increasingly experience the pleasure of design in airline lounges, on planes, in hotels and restaurants, and in their pockets as they listen to their favourite music being played on the symbol of the new design aesthetic.

Design is the new passion.

24

The Message is the Medium

Media and new technology pervade every part of our lives, and every day they become more omnipresent and yet less noticeable: movies-on-demand appear on our laptops; the device formerly known as a mobile phone becomes our new computer; VoIP enables us to talk to anyone, anywhere, in the world either free or for a few cents per hour; and the Internet allows us to live and work anywhere we choose. Never before has the social fabric changed so fast and so comprehensively.

Many of us can remember the introduction of the fax in the 1970s. That's right, the 1970s! Only 30-something years ago. And if you still have an old fax machine plugged in, count the number of times you go to it in a week, and compare that to the number of times you send an email or SMS.

The rate of progress may have been spectacular to date, but we haven't seen anything yet. The speed of computing technology just keeps increasing, and the opportunities created by the Web just keep expanding. According to Moore's Law, developed by Intel co-founder Gordon Moore in 1965, the number of transistors on a chip doubles every 24 months, and it continues to be the guiding principle of the high-tech industry. Computing speed doubles every two years.

Our reliance on the Web is profound. The non-technically minded amongst us marvel at things like how a plane stays up there, or how they get cranes onto the tops of buildings, and how it is that the Web doesn't crash. Imagine that.

Well, the stakes get higher each day. We have now entered the era of the Internet known as Web 2.0, where the emphasis has shifted from information silos to information initiatives, as control moves from the few to the many. The avatar of Web 2.0 is the weblog or blog, that individually controlled and intensely personalised version of a website. The millions of blogs that constitute the 'blogosphere' have created an alternative business model to traditional media and even to traditional Internet commerce. A new blog is created every second, so there are more than 80,000 blogs created every day or 30 million each year. The blogosphere continues to double about every five months.

This blog phenomenon highlights the overriding principle of Web 2.0: 'data democracy'. Web 2.0 can best be characterised by its sense of community, by individuals not only being in control of their own information sources (Web 1.0) but now being in control of their own information dissemination. We are witnessing people interacting with each other rather than with channels of technology.

According to Anya Kamenetz (*Fast Company*, June 2006, p. 68), personal connections being forged through words, pictures, video, and audio posted just for the hell of it are the life of the new Web, bringing together an estimated 60 million bloggers, 72 million MySpace users, and millions more on single-use social networks where people share one category of stuff, like Flickr (photos), Del.icio.us (links), Digg (news stories), *Wikipedia* (encyclopaedia), and YouTube (video).

Bradley Horowitz, head of technology development for Yahoo!, says, 'Social networking isn't a product or, God forbid, a company, but a feature that lives in service of some other mission.' TagWorld founder Evan Rifkin believes, 'User-generated content on the Internet will dramatically increase … we don't think this is a coolness issue. We believe people want to live their lives online.'

Technology and the communities created by the Internet are fuelling the spread of so-called minipreneurs. Early in 2006, Trendwatching.com cited the British example of Scoopt, a then three-month-old 'civic media press agency' that helps consumers sell photographs and videos of newsworthy events to the media. More than 1500 people in 35 countries have become members of Scoopt. Scoopt, which may or may not succeed as a business model, provides a rich example of the minipreneur.

However, as digital democracy increasingly touches our lives, what is happening to the traditional media and the new media that is already part of our daily activities? And where is it going in Australia?

The first answer links back to the explosion of digital democracy. Given that 98 per cent of NEOs are online and online frequently, NEOs are driving the changes to our traditional media in Australia as they replace conventional information sources with the Internet and mobile phones.

The future of the media market in Australia therefore looks nothing like the present. Traditional media including newspapers, commercial radio, magazines, and commercial free-to-air television are struggling in contrast to the extraordinary rise of the Internet as a serious contender for dominance of our lives and of the $10 billion Australian advertising industry as it heads into its biggest shake-up in living memory.

Newspapers, in their traditional form, will continue to struggle with a decline in readership. However, significant opportunities exist in the area of inserted colour magazines, as well as special-interest sections and Internet-connected content.

Magazines and newspapers together have the potential to work well for NEOs. High-NEO newspaper titles like the *Sydney Morning Herald* will survive and even thrive as they reinvent themselves for a world increasingly dominated by online news services.

Cinema is in decline, but still provides a useful secondary channel for reaching NEOs.

Radio is in recovery, and some interesting opportunities are emerging in radio, such as podcasting with deep appeal to the NEO market.

Commercial free-to-air television is failing to make up ground in the battle for the attention of NEOs and the all-important NEO dollar. Subscription or pay TV continues to provide more appeal to the demanding NEO market.

Let's review the media landscape in more detail to identify the major trends:

Magazines

The Australian magazine sector—both newsstand and newspaper-inserted—needs some good news, and the news is, well, OK. The magazine sector can expect, in the trend towards individualised information, a reversal of its gradual slide; in the case of specific titles, there is potential for good lifts in readership. The worst may be over for smart players in the magazine industry.

While magazine readership declines in the general population (down 1 per cent to 86 per cent), the drift has been arrested in the powerful NEO market (up 1 per cent to 91 per cent).

More specialist magazines and a stronger focus on quality,

particularly in lifestyle categories, are generating this NEO-led recovery.

Newspapers

The decline in newspaper readership has also slowed. However, competition from the booming Internet sector and, increasingly, specialised magazines will create continuing challenges and opportunities for publishers and editors. The future of newspapers is not as gloomy as some would have us believe. Granted, between 2000 and 2006 heavy newspaper readership (of seven papers or more a week) in the general population slipped from 33 per cent to 31 per cent, and NEO heavy readership fell from 41 per cent to 37 per cent. However, it appears to have stabilised.

The recovery of Melbourne's *Sunday Age* under the leadership of Alan Oakley, and the clear lessons to be learned from that recovery, draws a positive line in the sand for Australia's newspaper market. Oakley subsequently became the most influential newspaper editor in Australia by taking the helm at the *Sydney Morning Herald*, where he immediately initiated a project to design and produce the next generation of newspaper.

Newspaper-inserted Magazines

Magazines as inserts in newspapers continue to go from strength to strength, with NEOs approximately twice as likely as anyone else to read the *Australian Financial Review* magazine, the Fairfax *Sydney* and *Melbourne* magazines, *Good Weekend*, and the *Australian* magazine. This is not just a positive trend for newspapers; it is a permanent fixture in the future health of the sector.

Many in the paid-magazine sector believe the commercial success of inserted magazines is due to the lack of a cover price; distribution convenience; and, in some cases, the attraction to advertisers of being able to target just those lucrative markets of Sydney and Melbourne rather than the whole of the country.

Qualitative research that we have conducted has, however, shown that it is the quality of editorial direction of, for example, the *AFR* Magazine and the *Sydney* magazine that makes them so attractive to NEOs and, as a consequence, to commercially focused premium advertisers.

Commercial Television

Mark Twain famously said that rumours of his death were greatly exaggerated; and while the same could be said today of free-to-air (FTA) television in Australia, no new life is expected from the sector. Over the coming years, changes in commercial television market-share will be confined to the moving of slices of a static pie between the FTA networks.

FTA commercial television in Australia has barely changed its market size since 2000. Over that period, heavy TV viewing (defined as 4+ hours per day) has dropped a mere half a per cent to 19 per cent of the Australian population. Over the same period, heavy TV viewing by NEOs dropped 2 per cent to 11 per cent, and is more or less stable.

Subscription TV, another thorn in the side of FTA networks, is growing and will attract an increasing proportion of advertising in the future. NEOs like subscription TV because it gives them more control over their own programming options and, as a consequence, are 22 per cent more likely than anyone else to subscribe. And as the market matures, advertisers chasing the NEO dollar will be drawn to this medium to reach and motivate them with increasingly creative television commercials.

Commercial Radio

While commercial radio has the lowest penetration of any medium in the heavy media landscape, it has demonstrated weak signs of improvement. Since 2000, Australia's heavy commercial radio listening (4+ hours per day) has dropped to 17 per cent, and by 2006 had recovered by only 1 per cent. Significantly for commercial radio, however, the recovery in the NEO market has been more dramatic, with a 2 per cent recovery. Given that NEOs are 24 per cent of the population, that 2 per cent NEO lift may well account for the entire increase in the population as a whole.

Potentially, this bodes well for commercial radio, and reflects the increasing number of NEO knowledge workers listening in cars and in home offices. It also reflects the importance of both rich information and accessible entertainment to influential NEOs.

Cinema

Heavy cinema-visitation (2+ visits in last three months) is a perfect example of the power of NEOs as a lead indicator of market trends. After hitting a high in 2002 of 49 per cent, heavy cinema-visitation by NEOs slipped by 2 per cent in 2005. And then the slide hit the general population over the next year.

Much has been written about competition from DVDs and downloaded movies hitting cinema attendances. However, cinema is still a powerful medium. Almost half of all NEOs in the heavy-visitation category place cinema at the top of their traditional-media list—only the Internet has a better score.

It is often claimed that a lack of blockbusters caused the slump. However, it is the NEOs' continuing decline in interest that sets the real challenge for the future.

The Internet

The Internet is the stellar performer, and its future is now certain. With all traditional media flat or in decline, the one medium withstanding the trend is the Internet.

Rich content, followed by rich media and animated technology, has attracted rich advertisers to the online market, which in Australia tops $500 million. It is expected to surge to 10 per cent of the total advertising spend in Australia, pushing it past both the radio and magazine sectors' share of the advertising pie.

In the general population, heavy Internet use (8+ times in past week) has more than doubled since 2000 from 11 per cent to 28 per cent. In yet another example of the influence of NEOs on the rest of the population, NEOs' heavy use of the Internet started at 28 per cent in 2000 (the level it took the general population five years to reach) and soared to almost 60 per cent by 2005–06.

Forty-four per cent of NEOs have a broadband Internet connection at home compared to only 18 per cent of non-NEOs. Significantly for the media industry, half of all high-spending NEOs use the Internet for research, shopping, and paying bills—all activities that either provide a medium for advertising or that are of themselves commercial.

The dominance of the Internet not only has commercial influence on the economy, but also impacts traditional media. Of the general population, 9 per cent read newspapers and magazines less, as a direct consequence of Internet use, compared to 14 per cent of NEOs. The impact on television is more dramatic, with 13 per cent of the population and 23 per cent of NEOs watching less television as a direct consequence of Internet use.

Mobiles

The surprise growth will come from what currently passes for a mobile phone. Two years ago, it was very useful as a way for people to talk to each other—in exactly the same way that the Internet was a useful way of sending emails. And what happened to the Internet?

In the next few years, mobiles will transform from phones with novelty cameras to interactive gateways for 3G network operators, video television broadcasters, content publishers, content producers, and ... advertisers.

Broadband TV is already able to rapidly and cost-effectively deliver rich media services across PCs, mobile devices, and advanced digital television. In the UK, mobile-phone company 3 is set to become the world's first operator to sell airtime on its own network to advertisers, opening up its 3.2 million British customers to targeted marketing and advertising campaigns.

As the 3G platform rolls out across the mobile phones of Australia, mobile media is destined to become a major player in the commercial media landscape. The impact of the Internet on traditional media is now the stuff of legend. Mobiles will be the next big hit.

Changes to the media sector in Australia will be significant in the future and, to reiterate, the future looks nothing like the present. Media channels are changing, and dominance is shifting from traditional media. However, as broadband dominates and rich content and rich media proliferate, and as digital democracy sweeps the world, Marshall McLuhan's message that the medium is the message reverses. The message is the new king.

The message is the medium.

Conclusion

NEOs are already influencing how we live, work, and play. They dominate economic and political life in Australia through their individual activism and self-determinism.

Traditionals are also with us and are no less influential. They are not determining the future social fabric in the same way as NEOs, but our society and our economy cannot exist without Traditionals. They are the backbone of the economy. NEOs are its beating heart.

NEOs and Traditionals are completely different, and their difference is maintained over time. NEOs don't become like Traditionals, and Traditionals have no aspiration to be anything like NEOs. Certainly, some of their behaviours evolve; however, that's about it. Attitudes are very slow to change, and values tend to stay fixed.

An example of behavioural change can be found in the banking sector. A few years ago, telephone banking was a very NEO thing to do, and Traditionals wouldn't touch it. A couple of years later, both used telephone banking equally, and it failed to differentiate or discriminate between them. Then it became Internet banking that demonstrated the chasm in behaviour between NEOs and Traditionals.

All behaviour evolves and changes as, for example, we

become more comfortable with new technology and abandon old technology. Accordingly, we adjust the NEO typology every year to take account of those changes.

So, in short, NEOs and Traditionals are different and stay different over time. Both evolve and change, but their difference is maintained. And each type is valuable to the economy.

When it comes to marketing, however, the difference between NEOs and Traditionals becomes significant. Marketers in every sector, other than those selling basic-needs goods and services, must understand and market to NEOs. NEOs are changing the face of marketing. Just look at the iPod advertisements to see what impact NEOs are having on the marketing sector. Or look at a David Jones catalogue. Or go online and marvel at the changed ways we now discover products and services.

And it's not just in the consumer world that the difference between NEOs and Traditionals is important. In the workplace, managers are recognising that they have two different but equally valuable types of employee. Different workplace strategies are required for each type—different recruitment strategies, different training, different benefit packaging, different communications strategies, and different ways of recognising and valuing employees.

NEOs and Traditionals are equally important in Australian society. However, NEOs are powering the economy and redefining the workplace, the home, and the Third Space.

NEO power spans the market, the workplace, the political arena, and the media. A successful future awaits those who can recalibrate their social compass to map the changes underpinning the new economic order—and then change with them.

Appendix

NEOs, Traditionals, and Evolvers at a Glance

NEOs

1. NEOs are high discretionary-choice consumers rather than basic-needs consumers.
2. Twenty-four per cent of the population, NEOs account for more than half (54 per cent) of the discretionary spending in the economy.
3. They have higher spending propensity than anyone else and, as a consequence, consume constantly.
4. NEOs also have the highest spending capacity—they earn more than anyone else, so can fuel their constant consumption.
5. They have a sense of investment when they buy—a bargain for a NEO is *'something that is cheaper today than it will be tomorrow'*, rather than *'something that is cheaper today than it was yesterday'*.
6. While everyone wants the best price, NEOs have low confidence that discounts and price offers will *automatically* deliver the quality experience they expect.
7. NEOs are attracted first by the product and the experience it will deliver—price is just *'the cost'* of satisfying a deep desire.

8. They will focus on price only when they have low involvement with a purchase—when *desire* is not in play.

9. They have a preference for premium-lifestyle products—the well-designed, high-quality products at the top of every merchandise category.

10. For NEOs, food and beverage experiences go well beyond basic needs, way past mere sustenance, to a place where food is no longer fuel but something unusual and extraordinary; to where they experience exciting differences and uncertainties.

11. NEOs are inconspicuous consumers—brands are *secrets* to be *whispered* to themselves and to others who share their values, rather than external symbols of who they are or what they do.

12. NEOs love provenance—the story behind the person behind the product.

13. They have a high appetite for all kinds of rich information and rich content—they read more, know more, expect more, and will pay more.

14. They are more willing than anyone else to try something new, to *take the path least travelled.*

15. NEOs seek out the authentic, and are attracted to the hand-made; to products that '*stand for something*'; to merchandise created with personal commitment and passion.

16. They have a high appetite for brand relationship (a connection with their own values) rather than brand architecture (the promotion of corporate values).

17. NEOs are motivated by options—they like to discover something for themselves and then tell other NEOs about it (*word of mouth* and *word of web*).

18. NEOs are individualists with a high locus of

control — they believe success is determined by planning rather than by luck.

19. They regularly use, and are comfortable with, the internet—indeed they are happy to adopt new technology, but only when it delivers a service that matches their expectations and aspirations.

20. They cross all age barriers, but are more highly represented in the 20s, 30s, and 40s age-profiles.

21. NEOs prefer relationship marketing to mass marketing.

22. NEOs are heavy readers of magazines and newspapers, medium viewers of commercial television, and light listeners to commercial radio.

23. They are attracted to specialist magazines that focus on desire, imagination, design, whispered secrets, future directions, and that 'take a position' (for example: *Australian Gourmet Traveller*, *Belle*, *Wallpaper*, *AFR Magazine*, *Boss*, and *Sydney Magazine*).

24. They are socially active, have a strong sense of social and ethical responsibility, and like to convince others of their opinions.

25. NEOs believe strongly in the concept of learning a living rather than earning a living.

Traditionals

1. Traditionals are occasional consumers, motivated by calendar and promotional events.
2. Fifty per cent of the population, Traditionals account for less than a quarter (23 per cent) of discretionary spending in the economy.
3. They have low spending propensity and, as a consequence, consume intermittently.
4. Traditionals are attracted to 'the deal', and motivated by discounts and price offers.
5. They have a preference for function ahead of design; cost ahead of lasting quality.
6. They tend to be conspicuous consumers—branded products are external symbols of who they are or what they do.
7. Traditionals prefer the tried-and-true ahead of the new and challenging.
8. Brands to a Traditional are a shortcut to certainty, and symbols of belonging.
9. Wealthy Traditionals will buy luxury products, but do so infrequently.
10. They have a low locus of control, and tend to believe life is determined by luck rather than any action they can take to influence outcomes.
11. Traditionals are slower to adopt new technology, with lower percentages of Traditionals using the internet regularly.
12. They cross all age barriers, but are more highly represented in the 50-plus age-profiles.
13. Traditionals prefer mass marketing and mass communication.

Evolvers

1. Evolving consumers are most like NEOs.
2. Frequently, Evolvers experience consumer conflict because they recognise the quality that attracts NEOs, but don't like paying the price (more like Traditionals).
3. In general, Evolvers are motivated by messages and experiences that attract NEOs.
4. Evolvers are not as economically valuable as NEOs, but are more valuable than Traditionals.

Acknowledgements

The authors enthusiastically acknowledge the personal and professional contribution made by Michele Levine, the chief executive officer of Roy Morgan Research, and the role played by Gary Morgan in the alliance partnership that the authors enjoy with Roy Morgan Research internationally. We also thank those key staff members at Roy Morgan Research who, over five years, have contributed to the international success of the NEO typology.

We also acknowledge KPMG generally, and former chairman David Crawford specifically, for providing us with the platform upon which we were originally able to identify the most valuable consumers in the world.

We also wish to pay tribute to those executives and business entrepreneurs across Australia who had the imagination to take on something as new and exciting as the NEO typology and who, by creating their own success, transformed it into the new consumer currency. And we also wish to express our appreciation to those opinion leaders such as the splendid Robert Gottliebsen who, for so many years, have supported our insights and ideas.

We have been blessed to work with outstanding alliance partners, including Fleur Brown and Antonia O'Neil, two of

Australia's best media and marketing strategists; Sir Richard Heygate in London, who enthusiastically took the NEO challenge to the UK business world; and New York business strategist Stephani Cook, who was the first to identify the international value of our methodology.

Thanks, also, to Henry Rosenbloom and his team at Scribe for their highly professional approach to publishing what we consider to be the right book at the right time. A small percentage of material in this book is drawn from our first book, *I-Cons*. It has been updated and is reproduced with the permission of Random House.

A huge tribute to John Ashby, the indefatigable chairman of our consulting firm, the NEO Group, who always makes sense when common sense seems anything but common.

And finally, we give great thanks to our personal partners, Dr Greer Honeywill and Maarten Briede, for their guidance and support throughout our journey.

Special Note: Roy Morgan Research

NEO data and statistics in this book are, unless otherwise identified, sourced from the NEO typology on the Roy Morgan Research Single Source database.